HOW TO WIN THE CULTURE WAR

A CHRISTIAN
BATTLE PLAN FOR A
SOCIETY IN CRISIS

PETER KREEFT

InterVarsity Press
Downers Grove, Illinois

InterVarsity Press
P.O. Box 1400, Downers Grove, IL 60515-1426
World Wide Web: www.ivpress.com
E-mail: mail@ivpress.com

InterVarsity Press® is the book-publishing division of InterVarsity Christian Fellowship/USA®, a student movement active on campus at hundreds of universities, colleges and schools of nursing in the United States of America, and a member movement of the International Fellowship of Evangelical Students. For information about local and regional activities, write Public Relations Dept., InterVarsity Christian Fellowship/USA, 6400 Schroeder Rd., P.O. Box 7895, Madison, WI 53707-7895, or visit the IVCF website at <www.ivcf.org>.

Cover illustration: Roberta Polfus

ISBN 0-8308-2316-6

Printed in the United States of America ∞

Library of Congress Cataloging-in-Publication Data

Kreeft, Peter.
  How to win the culture war: a Christian battle plan for a society in crisis/Peter Kreeft.
    p.   cm.
  ISBN 0-8308-2316-6 (pbk.: alk. paper)
  1. Christianity and culture. 2. Social values—United States.
3. Virtues. 4. United States—Moral conditions—20th century. I. Kreeft, Peter.
II. Title.
BR115.C8 .K65 2002
261—dc 21   2002017271

P	18	17	16	15	14	13	12	11	10	9	8	7	6	5
Y	16	15	14	13	12	11	10	09	08	07	06	05		

For James Dobson, Richard John Neuhaus and Alan Keyes.
the Eisenhower, Churchill and MacArthur of World War III.

CONTENTS

Introduction.........9

1. WE ARE AT WAR
A Wake-Up Call.........13

2. THE IDENTITY OF OUR ENEMY
Principalities & Powers.........24

3. THE KIND OF WAR WE ARE IN
True & False Spiritual Warfare.........32

4. THE FUNDAMENTAL PRINCIPLE OF
ALL CULTURE WARS
Colson's Law.........46

5. OUR ENEMY'S BATTLE PLAN
Satan's Strategy for the Third Millennium.........55

6. THE FIERCEST BATTLE
Sex Wars.........88

7. THE SECRET WEAPON THAT WILL
WIN THE WAR
Saints.........100

8. BASIC TRAINING
How to Be a Saint.........107

9. THE PROGNOSIS FOR VICTORY
Why We Must Win.........118

Introduction

There is one thing that almost everybody in America agrees about. Liberals and conservatives, rich and poor, atheists and theists, labor and management, women and men, gay and straight, prolife and prochoice, capitalists and socialists—just about everybody with a nose agrees that our culture is in what one president called "deep doo-doo."

Different groups have different explanations for the problem. Conservatives blame liberals, and liberals blame conservatives. Straights blame gays, and gays blame straights. Whites blame blacks, and blacks blame whites. Men blame women, and women blame men.

Some say that there's no one to blame, that it just happens. That's the purest pessimism of all. It means there's nothing anybody can do about it. So America is doomed, for if nobody broke America, nobody can fix it. If there's no cause, there's no cure.

Americans have never believed that before, except for Stoics, fatalists, Calvinists and Boston Red Sox fans. (Definition of a Red Sox fan: someone who comes to opening day with a sign that says, "Wait Till Next Year.") Most Americans have always thought that human problems have human causes and human solutions—at least these kinds of problems.

What kinds? Polls keep showing that the problems most Americans worry about most deeply are not political or economic but social issues, cultural issues, in fact moral issues. These are the issues that most directly affect the lives of ordinary people and families: drugs, terrorism, divorce, homelessness, rape, alcoholism, violence, child abuse, abortion, the destruction of families, teen pregnancies, AIDS, suicide. We're more worried about our wrongs than our rights.

This is obvious to anyone but an academic. How could a mother be more concerned with the Gross National Product than with whether her daughter is going to be raped?

No wonder we're having fewer children. Who wants to bring babies into a battlefield? Only the heroic or the naive.

Nobody makes a TV show about kids today with a title like *Happy Days*. The fifties were far from utopia, but we all know they were significantly happier than today.

At this point someone will respond by quoting the ultimate law of life: "Ah, but you can't turn back the clock. You can't go home again. You can't stop progress."

Yes, you can. This "ultimate law" is a lie. You *can* turn a clock back, both literally and figuratively. And you'd better, if the clock is keeping bad time. A clock or a society is a manmade invention. It doesn't just happen, like the weather. We invented it, we can break it, and we can fix it.

We *can* stop this false god Progress. But instead we have stopped real progress. Real progress means getting closer to your goal. And the goal of every human being is happiness. Whatever we do, we do to obtain some kind of happiness.

And since we are no longer in "happy days," it logically follows that we have stopped progressing, by the most universal definition of "progress"—progress toward happiness. We have regressed.

So when people today, with glum, stoical faces, say, "You can't stop progress," they really mean exactly the opposite: you can't stop regress.

I say you can. And I want to tell you how.

But first, who am I to tell you? I am not a sociologist. (Sometimes I think I would rather be a salamander than a sociologist.) I am not an "expert" in anything. What qualifies me to write this book, then? Precisely that: that I am not an "expert." It's the "experts" who are the problem. And it's the rest of us, those who still rely on common sense, who can solve them. "Common sense" means the practical sense that is common to everybody *except* the "experts."

It's high time for us nonexperts, us amateurs, to take over. It's high time for our democracy to become democratic.

To do that, we need to do something truly radical. But it won't cost a cent or a drop of blood. We need to ignore the experts and listen to common sense instead. That will make the experts really mad. Experts can't stand to be ignored.

In fact, this book will offend many people, for the same reason it will delight many others: because it is not only *about* a war—a "culture war," a spiritual war, a jihad—but it is itself an *act* of war. It will thus offend two kinds of people. First, it will offend the "experts." (It's already done that.) Second, it will offend people who hate to be told there is a war. These are *terribly nice* people—Canadians, for instance. This book will probably be censored in Canada as "hate speech," like Dr. Laura, and be confiscated at the border.

It's loud and crude, and I'm not sorry. For it is written on a battlefield, in the heat of battle. It is written for soldiers or potential soldiers, enlistees. It is therefore not a carefully researched, beautifully nuanced, politely academic argument. It is not a sweet violin; it is an ugly, blaring trumpet. On a battlefield, a trumpet works better than a violin.

Here is a preview and summary of the book in one page.

To win any war, and any kind of war, the nine most necessary things to know are the following:

1. that you are at war
2. who your enemy is
3. what kind of war you are in
4. what the basic principle of this kind of war is
5. what the enemy's strategy is
6. where the main battlefield is
7. what weapon will defeat the enemy
8. how to acquire this weapon
9. why you will win

You cannot win a war

1. if you blissfully sew peace banners on a battlefield
2. if you do not know who you are fighting
3. if you do not know what kind of war you are fighting
4. if you do not know the basic rules of battle
5. if you do not know your enemy's battle plan
6. if you send your troops to the wrong battlefield
7. if you use the wrong weapons
8. if you do not know how to get the right weapon
9. if you are not confident of your inevitable victory

This little book is a basic, practical nine-point checklist to be sure we know this minimum, at least.

1

WE ARE AT WAR
A WAKE-UP CALL

I assume you would not be buying, or browsing through, a book with the title *How to Win the Culture War* if you believed "God's in his heaven, all's right with the world." If you are surprised to be told that our entire civilization is in crisis, I welcome you back to earth and hope you had a nice vacation on the moon.

Many minds do seem moonstruck. Especially those of the so-called intellectuals, who are supposed to have their eyes more open, not less. Most of them are the bland leading the bland. After a lifetime in academia, I have discovered that there is only one requirement for someone to actually believe any of the one hundred most absurd ideas possible for a human mind to conceive: you must be an intellectual. Some ideas are so ridiculous that only a Ph.D. could believe them.

For instance, take *Time* magazine. (Please! Thoreau said,

sagely, of a similarly named publication, "Read not the *Times*; read the eternities.") A cover article in *Time* a few years ago was about the question "Why is everything getting better?" Why is life so good in America today? Why does everybody feel so satisfied and optimistic about the quality of life? The authors never once questioned the assumption; they only wondered why.

It turned out, upon reading the article, that every single aspect of life they mentioned, every reason why everything was getting better and better, was economic. People have more money. Period. End of discussion.

Except the poor, of course. But they don't count, because they don't write *Time* magazine. They don't even read it.

I have a theory about *Time*: that it is simply *Playboy* with clothes on. For one kind of playboy, the world is simply one big whorehouse; for another kind, it's one big piggy bank. For both kinds of playboy, things are getting better and better.

That's why Americans gave a 75 percent approval rating to Bill Clinton, the perfect combination of the two kinds of playboy. He kept himself happy with some big whores, and he kept us happy with some big piggy banks. We loved him for the same reason the Germans loved Hitler when they elected him: "It's the economy, stupid." Hitler gave them autobahns and Volkswagens, jobs and housing. In fact, Hitler wrought the greatest economic miracle of the twentieth century: from economic and military ruin to full employment and national pride in a few short years. What else matters as long as the emperor gives you bread and circuses? People are pigs, not saints; they love slops, not holiness, right? Or wrong?

Sexual pigginess and economic pigginess are natural twins. For *lust* and *greed* are almost interchangeable words. In fact,

America does not know the difference between sex and money. It treats sex like money because it treats sex as a medium of exchange, and it treats money like sex because it expects its money to get pregnant and reproduce.

There is one little problem with the pig philosophy, however, and it is intensely practical: death. Both sex and money are often fatal. Two words show that: AIDS and suicide.

Most Americans are "sexually active." (Next to technology, euphemism is our greatest achievement.) Half of all "sexually active" people have some sexually transmitted disease. Many STDs are incurable. Some are fatal.

Suicide is certainly the most in-your-face index of unhappiness there is. And suicide is almost always directly proportionate to wealth. The richer you and your country are, the more likely it is that you will find life so good that you will choose to blow your brains out. Suicide among preadults has increased 5,000 *percent* since the "happy days" of the fifties. If suicide is not an index of crisis, especially of the coming generation, what is?

But there are more suicides than that. Half of all marriages commit suicide. That is what divorce is—the suicide of the new "one flesh" made by the marriage. If half of all the citizens of a country committed suicide, would you think that country had a bright future or a happy present? But the citizens of any country are not merely individuals; they are also families. Individuals are not the primary building blocks of societies; families are. Individuals are the building blocks of families. So half of all the new citizens of America commit suicide.

And if you insist on limiting "new citizens" to "individual children conceived," the statistics are not much better. One-third of all American children are killed—by their mothers, before they can be born, using healers as hit men.

This is a happy country? This is peace?

I know a doctor who spent two years in the Congo winning the confidence of a dying tribe who would not trust outsiders (black or white) and who were dying because of their bad diet. He was a dietitian, and he saved their lives. Once they knew this, they trusted him totally and asked him all sorts of questions about life in the West. They believed all the amazing things he told them, like flying to the moon and destroying whole cities with one bomb, but there were two things they literally could not believe. One was that in the West there are atheists—people who believe in no gods at all. ("Are these people blind and deaf? Have they never seen a leaf or heard a waterfall?") The other was that in one nation alone (America), over a million mothers each year pay doctors to kill their babies before they are born. Their reaction to this was to giggle, which was their embarrassed way of trying to be polite, assuming it was a joke. They simply had no holding place in their minds for this concept, and they expected every day that the doctor would tell them the point of the joke.

And it is we who call these people "primitive." The irony is mountainous.

Mother Teresa said, simply (everything she said, she said simply), "When a mother can kill her baby, what is left of civilization to save?" Chuck Colson has said that a "new Dark Ages" is looming. It is a darkness that began by calling itself the "Enlightenment" at its birth three centuries ago. And this brave new world has proved to be only a cowardly old dream.

We were warned. We had true prophets as well as false: Kierkegaard, 150 years ago, in *The Present Age*. Spengler, 85 years ago, in *The Decline of the West*. Chesterton, who wrote 75 years ago that "the next great heresy is going to be simply an attack on morality, and especially sexual morality. . . . The madness of tomorrow is not in Moscow but in Manhattan." Huxley, 65 years ago, in *Brave New World*. David Riesman, 45 years ago, in *The Lonely Crowd*. C. S. Lewis, 55 years ago, in *The Abolition of Man*. Romano Guardini, 50 years ago, in *The End of the Modern World*. Solzhenitsyn, 25 years ago, in his Harvard commencement address. And John Paul the Great, the greatest man in the worst century in history, who has even more chutzpah than Ronald Reagan—who dared to call *them* "the evil empire"—by calling *us* "the culture of death." That's *our* culture, and his, including Italy, which now has the lowest birth rate in the entire world, and Poland, which now seems to be about to share in the rest of the West's abortion holocaust.

It does not take much of a gift of prophecy to forecast where this road leads. It takes only minimal biblical literacy—an increasingly rare commodity in the West.

If the God of life does not respond to this culture of death with judgment, then God is not God. If God does not honor the blood of the hundreds of millions of innocent victims of this culture of death, then the God of the Bible, the God of Abraham, the God of Israel, the God of the prophets, the God of orphans and widows, the Defender of the defenseless, is a man-made myth, a fairy tale, an ideal as insubstantial as a dream.

But (you may object) is not the God of the Bible merciful and forgiving?

He is indeed. But the unrepentant refuse forgiveness. And forgiveness, being a gift, must be freely given and freely received. How can it be received by a moral relativist who denies that there is anything to forgive except unforgiveness, nothing to judge but judgmentalism? How can a Pharisee or a pop psychologist be saved?

But is not the God of the Bible compassionate?

Indeed he is. But he is not compassionate to the demons worshiped by the Canaanites who "make [their] children pass through the fire" (Ezekiel 20:31). Perhaps *your* God is compassionate to this work of human sacrifice—the God of your demands, the God of your "religious preference." But if so, he is certainly not the God of the Bible. Look at the data. Read the Book.

But is not the God of the Bible revealed most fully and finally in the New Testament rather than the Old? In sweet and gentle Jesus rather than wrathful and warlike Jehovah?

The opposition is heretical; it is the old heresy of Marcion in modern form, a heresy as immortal as the demons who inspired it. Our data refute this heresy—our live data, which is divine data and talking data, and thus his name is "the Word of God." This data refuted the heretical hypothesis in question when he said, "The Father and I are one" (John 10:30). The opposition between nice Jesus and nasty Jehovah denies the very essence of Christianity: Christ's identity as the Son of God. For let's remember our biology as well as our theology: like father, like son. *That* Jesus is no more the Son of *that* God than Barney is the son of Hitler.

Will the real Jesus please stand up? He does so gladly. The Gospels are pop-up books: open their pages and he leaps out. Let's dare to look at our data; let's see what sweet and gentle Jesus actually said about the sins of the Canaanites, about their culture of death. Many centuries ago those Canaanites used to perform their liturgies of human sacrifice, their infanticidal devotions to the devil, in the valley of Gehenna, just outside the holy city of Jerusalem. It was a vast abortuary—like our culture. When the people of God entered the Promised Land, the Prince of Peace commanded them to kill the supernatural cancer of the Canaanites. Even after that was done, the Jews would not dare to live in that accursed valley. They used it only to burn their garbage. The devil's promised land became a garbage dump for God's people. And the fires never went out, day or night. (No matches.)

Sweet and gentle Jesus chose this place—Gehenna—as his image for hell. And he told many of the leaders of his chosen people that they were headed there and were leading many others there with them. He said to them, "Truly, truly I say to you, the IRS lawyers and White House interns go into the kingdom of God before you do" (modern "dynamic equivalence" and "contemporary relevance" translation). He said, "If any of you put a stumbling block before one of these little ones who believe in me, it would be better for you if a great millstone were hung around your neck and you were thrown into the sea" (Mark 9:42).

That is our data. That is the real Jesus. And that is the Jesus who is "the same yesterday and today and forever" (Hebrews 13:8). He has not started manufacturing Styrofoam millstones.

But isn't it true that "God is love" (1 John 4:16)? God is a lover, not a warrior, right?

No, God is a lover who is a warrior. The question fails to understand what love is—what the love that God is, is. Love is at war with hate and betrayal and selfishness and all love's enemies. Love fights. Ask any parent. Yuppie love, like puppy love, may be merely "compassion," but mother love and father love is war. "God is love" indeed, but what kind of love? Back to our data: does the Bible call him "God the puppy" or "God the yuppie"? Or is it "God the Father"?

In fact, every page of his Book bristles with spear points, from Genesis 3 through Revelation 20. The road from paradise lost to paradise regained is soaked in blood. At the very center of the story is a cross—a symbol of conflict if there ever was one.

The theme of spiritual warfare is never absent in Scripture and never absent in the life and writings of a single canonized saint. But it is never present in the religious education of most of my "Catholic" college students. Whenever I speak of it, they are stunned and silent, as if they have suddenly entered another world.

They have. They have gone through the wardrobe to meet the Lion and the Witch, past the warm fuzzies, the fur coats of psychology disguised as religion, into the cold snows of Narnia, where the White Witch is the ruler of this world and Aslan is not a tame lion but a warrior—a world where they meet Christ the King, not Christ the kitten.

Welcome back from the moon, kids.

Who doesn't know we are at war? Who doesn't know the barbarians are at the gates—no, inside the gates, writing the scripts of the TV shows and movies, writing the public school textbooks and judicial decisions? Only the ones in the lunar bubble of academia or the lunar bubble of establishment religious education with the unprofitable prophets who cry, "Peace, peace," when there is no peace, the ones who compose those dreary, drippy little liberal lullabies we endure as "contemporary hymns."

But where is this culture of death coming from? Right here. America is the center of the culture of death. America is the world's one and only cultural superpower.

Do you know what pious Muslims call us? They call us "the Great Satan." (Impious Muslims call us that too, but that makes no difference; we are what we are.)

But America has the most just, most moral, most wise and most biblically based historical and constitutional foundation in the world.

Just like ancient Israel.

And America is one of the most religious countries in the world.

Just like ancient Israel.

And the Church is big and rich and free in America.

Just like ancient Israel.

If God still loves his Church in America, he will soon make it small and poor and persecuted, just as he did to ancient Israel, so that he can keep it alive, pruning it. If he loves us, he will cut the deadwood away, and we will bleed. Then the blood of the martyrs will be the seed of the Church again and a second spring will come, with new buds—but not without blood. It never happens without blood, without sacrifice, without suffering. Christ's work—if it is really Christ's work and not a comfortable counterfeit—never happens without Christ's cross. Whatever happens without the cross may be good work, but it is not Christ's work, for Christ's work is bloody. Christ's work is a blood transfusion. That is how salvation happens.

If we put gloves on our hands to avoid the splinters from the cross, if we practice safe spiritual sex, spiritual contraception, then his kingdom will not come and his will and work will not be done and our world will die.

I don't mean merely that Western civilization will die. That's a piece of trivia. I mean that eternal souls will die. Ramons and Vladimirs and Tiffanies and Bridgets will miss out on heaven. That's what's at stake in this war: not just whether America will become a banana republic or whether we'll forget Shakespeare or even whether some nuclear terrorist will incinerate half of humanity, but whether our children and our children's children will see God forever. That's why we must wake up and smell the corpses, the rotting souls, the dying children.

Knowing we are at war—at all times, but especially in such times as these—is the first prerequisite to winning it.

What difference does it make to know we are at war?

First of all, it means living in reality, not denial.

Second, it means having a chance to win it. (If one side knows it is at war and the other does not, which side do you think will win?)

Third, it means a radical change of consciousness, of perspective, of values. Imagine the shock of children running across springtime fields and chasing butterflies when they suddenly realize that it is a minefield, that what they mistook for butterflies are live bullets in the air. Wartime consciousness suddenly clicks in, with a very practical alertness and attention and also a very practical sense of perspective and sense of values. Little things no longer loom so large, and large things (life and death) no longer seem so little and far away. No one complains about lumpy beds on a battlefield or bleats about their "sexual needs" or worries about their stock options.

But (you may think) this is exaggeration: most of us are not really in the extreme danger of a literal battlefield, where it is being decided whether our bodies will live or die, where our whole lifetime is perilously poised over an abyss and where there are real enemies, real human persons, who are trying to kill us. This is true, but only because we are in the infinitely more extreme danger of a *spiritual* battlefield where it is being decided whether our souls will live or die, where our whole eternity is perilously poised over an abyss and where there are indeed real enemies who are trying to kill us—not just our bodies but our souls.

And that is the second necessary thing to know.

2

THE IDENTITY
OF OUR ENEMY
PRINCIPALITIES & POWERS

W e have been making some very stupid mistakes for very many years in answering the question "Who is our enemy?"

For almost half a millennium, Protestants and Catholics have thought of each other as the enemy, as the problem, and have addressed these "problems" by consigning each other's bodies to graves on battlefields and each other's souls to hell. Gradually the light dawned: Protestants and Catholics are not enemies but "separated brethren" fighting together against a common enemy.

Who is that enemy?

For almost two millennia, many Christians thought it was the Jews, and we did such Christless things to our fathers in the faith that we made it almost impossible for the Jews to see their God—the true God—in us.

Today, many Christians think it is the Muslims. But the Muslims are often more loyal to their merely human Christ than we are to our divine Christ, and they often live more godly lives following their fallible scriptures and their fallible prophet than we do following our infallible Scriptures and infallible Prophet. (One of the two systems must be fallible, for they are mutually contradictory. Either Jesus is a mere man or he is divine. Either the Qur'an is right and the New Testament is wrong about that, or vice versa.) If you compare the stability of the family and the safety of children among Muslims and among Christians in today's world; or if you compare the rate of abortion, divorce, adultery and sodomy among Muslims and among Christians in today's world; and if you dare to interpret this data by the principle announced by all the prophets of our own Scriptures when they say, repeatedly, that God blesses those who obey his laws and punishes those who do not; then I think you know one reason Islam is growing faster than Christianity today in the West. Christians and Muslims worship the same God and acknowledge the same divine commandments because we both learned of God and his commandments from the same source: God's own revelation to Abraham and his people the Jews. Faithful Muslims serve under the same divine General, though through a different and more primitive communications network. They can be our allies in the culture war, though they do not know the way of salvation, the Christ. They may be heretics, but they are not enemies. (Except of course, for the murderous few who make most of the news. To call terrorism "Islamic" is like calling the Inquisition "Christian." It is like calling a cannibal a chef.)

The same is true of the Mormons, the Quakers and the
Jehovah's Witnesses.

Some of us think our enemies are "the liberals" or "the liberal establishment." But for one thing, that term is so flexible
that it is almost meaningless. And for another thing, it's a
political term, not a religious one. Whatever is good or bad
about any of the forms of political liberalism, that is neither
the cause nor the cure of the spiritual cancer that makes this
culture war a spiritual one and a matter of life or death—eternal life or death, not merely economic or political life or
death. Whether Jack and Jill go up the hill to heaven or down
the hill to hell won't be decided by whether government wel-
fare checks increase or decrease.

Our enemies are not even the anti-Christian bigots who
hate us and want to kill us, whether these are Chinese com-
munist totalitarians who imprison and persecute Christians
or whether they are Sudanese Muslim terrorists who enslave
and murder Christians. They are our patients, not our enemies. They are the ones we are trying to save. We are Christ's
nurses. These patients think the nurses are their enemies, but
the nurses know better. Our word for them—Christ's word
for them—is "Father, forgive them; for they do not know
what they are doing" (Luke 23:34).

Our enemies are not even the canker worm within our
own culture, the media mouths of the culture of death: Larry
Flynt and Ted Turner and Howard Stern and AOL Time
Warner and Disney, who make missionary movies for the
Antichrist. They too are victims; they too are our patients,
though they hate our hospital and go running around poison-
ing other patients. But the poisoners are our patients too, for
whoever poisons was first poisoned himself. This is also true

of the gay and lesbian activists who desecrate, the feminist witches who blaspheme and the abortionists who murder. If we are what we claim to be—cells in Christ's body—then we do what he did to these people: we descend into their world and offer ourselves for their salvation, to the point of blood if necessary. We go into the gutters, as Mother Teresa did. Even though we do not all physically go into the gutters, as she did, yet we must all go into the spiritual gutters, for that is where the need is, that is where the spiritually dying are. Even though we do not all physically give our blood, yet in giving our time, we all give our life, for life is time—"lifetime." (Do not have children unless you understand that!)

Our enemies are not even the heretics within the Church, the cafeteria Christians, the à la carte Christians, the "I Did It My Way" Christians. (In Massachusetts we have "Kennedy Catholics" instead of Catholic Kennedys.) They are also our patients, though they are quislings. They are the deceived; they are the victims of our enemy; they are not our enemy.

Our enemies are not even the theologians in some so-called Christian seminaries and theology departments who have sold their souls for thirty pieces of scholarship and prefer the plaudits of their peers to the praise of their God. These Christophobes pull the claws from the Lion of the Tribe of Judah and dispense spiritual diaphragms and IUDs to their students for fear the living Christ will make their souls pregnant with his alarmingly active life. But they are not our enemies. They too are our patients.

Our enemies are not even the few really wicked priests and pastors and bishops and ministers, the abusive baby-sitters who corrupt Christ's little ones whom they swore to protect. They merit Christ's Millstone of the Month Award.

But they too are victims in need of healing.

Who, then, is our enemy?

Surely you have heard the answer at some time. All the saints through the Church's history have always given the same two answers, for they come from the same two sources: from the Word of God on paper and from the Word of God on wood, from every page of the New Testament and from Christ. They are the reason he went to the cross.

Yet these two answers are not well known. In fact, the first answer is almost never mentioned today outside so-called fundamentalist circles. Not once in my life can I recall ever hearing a sermon on it.

Our enemies are demons. Fallen angels. Evil spirits.

Our secular culture claims that anyone who believes this is at best an uneducated, narrow-minded bigot and at worst mentally deranged. Therefore, by this standard, Jesus Christ must have been one of the greatest bigots and madmen ever. For he taught it clearly, strongly, repeatedly and assiduously. "Do not fear those who kill the body, and after that can do nothing more. But I will warn you whom to fear: fear him who, after he has killed, has authority to cast into hell" (Luke 12:4-5).

I realize there is controversy among theologians about this verse, about who Jesus is talking about here, whether God or Satan. But I do not see how he can possibly be talking about God. God's work is to save souls, not to destroy them. Destroying souls in hell is the work of Satan, not God.

Jesus said to Peter, "Simon, Simon, listen! Satan has demanded to sift all of you like wheat" (Luke 22:31). Peter learned the lesson and passed it on to us in his first epistle: "Discipline yourselves, keep alert. Like a roaring lion your adversary the devil prowls around, looking for someone to devour. Resist him, steadfast in your faith" (1 Peter 5:8-9). Paul too knew that "our struggle is not against enemies of blood and flesh, but against the rulers, against the authorities, against the cosmic powers of this present darkness, against the spiritual forces of evil in the heavenly places" (Ephesians 6:12).

Pope Leo XIII saw this truth too. At the end of the nineteenth century he received a vision of the coming twentieth century that history has proved terrifyingly true. He saw Satan, at the beginning of time, allowed one century in which to do his worst work, and Satan chose the twentieth. This pope with the name and the heart of a lion was so overcome by the terror of this vision that he fell into a swoon like a Victorian lady. When he revived, he composed a prayer for the Catholic Church to use throughout this century of spiritual warfare:

> Saint Michael, archangel, defend us in battle. Be our protection against the wickedness and snares of the Devil. May God rebuke him, we humbly pray; and do thou, O prince of the heavenly host, by the power of God, thrust into hell Satan and all the evil spirits who roam through the world seeking the ruin of souls.

This prayer was known by every Catholic and prayed after every low Mass—until the 1960s. And that was exactly when the Catholic Church was struck with the incomparably swift disaster that has taken away half its priests, two-thirds of its nuns and nine-tenths of its children's theological and moral knowledge by turning the faith of our fathers into the doubts of our dissenters. It's been a diabolical reversal of Christ's first miracle at Cana, converting the wine of the gospel into the water of psychobabble, an antimiracle by the Antichrist.

I said there were *two* enemies. The second is even more horrible than the first. There is one nightmare even more terrifying than being chased by the devil, even being caught by the devil, even being tortured by the devil. That is the nightmare of *becoming* a devil. The horror outside your soul is terrible enough, but it is not as terrible as the horror inside your soul.

The horror inside our souls, of course, is sin. *Sin* is another word that, if any dares to speak it today, elicits only embarrassment from the Christian and condemnation from the secularist, who condemns only condemnations, judges only judgmentalism and believes that the only sin is believing in sin.

All sin is the devil's work, though he usually uses the flesh and the world as his instruments. Sin *means* doing the devil's work, tearing and damaging God's work. A*nd we do this*. We do it in each of our sins. That is the only reason why the devil can do his awful work in our world. God won't allow him to do it without our free consent.

And that is the deepest reason why the Church is weak and the world is dying.

But the corollary to this truth is even more hopeful than that truth itself is terrible. If sin is the enemy, then the Savior from sin is the answer, and he is infinitely more powerful than his enemy. The weapon that will win this war—this war's atomic bomb—is saints. For saints are not just very good people, humanly good people; saints are little Christs, flawed cells in Christ's flawless body. Sanctity is defined by Christ, not Christ by sanctity.

When the light of sanctity, that is, the light of Christ, meets the darkness of sin and the culture of death and its dark lord, what happens? When this light shines into this darkness, the darkness is not able to comprehend it, not able to surround it, either with understanding or with power. Satan cannot understand Christ's saints, and Satan cannot conquer Christ's saints.

But that is the ultimate, final truth. To get there, we need to explore aspects of the road. And the next aspect is what kind of war we are in. We already know it is spiritual warfare. But we often make a classic mistake about spiritual warfare—a mistake that has a long history associated with an error called Gnosticism, an error that began in the first century (the last few books of the New Testament combat it) and that is resurrecting powerfully in our time both inside and outside the Church. Instead of beginning by defining it abstractly, I begin the next chapter by presenting a typical concrete example of it that I encountered and that you will probably recognize as similar to what you've observed.

3

THE KIND OF WAR
WE ARE IN
TRUE & FALSE SPIRITUAL
WARFARE

The most popular religion in America is not Christianity. Nor is it atheism or materialism or scientism or secularism or naturalism. It is "spirituality."

"Spirituality" (in the popular sense of the word used in bookstore sections) is the current form of the oldest and largest and most immortal heresy in Christian history. Its old names were Gnosticism, Manichaeism and Marcionism. It is attractive because it denies the two answers given at the end of the previous chapter as to the identity of our enemies. It denies devils (saying that spirit is only good, not evil) and it denies sin (saying that man is only good, not evil). It confuses three things: man's true self, goodness and "spirituality."

Christianity unconfuses these three things. Christianity

identifies goodness not with "spirituality" but with sanctity or holiness or charity or obedience to God's will and law. And Christianity identifies man's self with body as well as soul (this is why sex is not indifferent but crucial) and with original sin as well as original goodness.

Let me tell you a little incident that provoked me to realize the immense difference between Christianity and "spirituality."

Harry (not his real name, but a real person) was an amateur philosopher and a professional fishing guide. We had booked him for some surf fishing instruction on Martha's Vineyard, and I had been enjoying conversation with him for hours, exchanging tips and recommendations on our favorite writers—until I mentioned C. S. Lewis. His face darkened. "Oh, *him!*" It was Harry's first negative comment of the day, the first writer he could not recommend.

"Why don't you like him?"

"Oh, he's a competent stylist, especially his fiction. Everybody loves his children's stories, it seems—the Narnia books. I just can't take his religious writing."

"What have you read by him?"

"*The Four Loves.*"

"Anything else?"

"A book called *Mere Christianity*, I think."

"And what don't you like about those two books?"

"I just don't like him, that's all."

"Well, what quality turned you off?"

"I just think he's not very *spiritual.*"

I was prepared for the commonest Lewisophobias: the secularist's fear of real religion, which he often meets for the first time in Lewis, or the leftist's fear of the very rational and human conservatism he also often meets for the first time in

Lewis. But this objection—"not very spiritual"—I had previously heard only from feet-far-off-the-ground New Agers, who always seemed to be flighty, flaky and female, at least in spirit. But Harry's life and loves were fish, rods and boats.

Further conversation with Harry revealed that he had been an alcoholic, a cocaine addict and a serial adulterer, and he told me of his past follies in a tone that sounded closer to nostalgia and pride than remorse or repentance. I suddenly realized that the most obvious difference between Christianity and "spirituality" is the fact that Christianity includes *commandments*, while "spirituality" includes only *values*.

Most of the upscale bookstores have created two separate sections, labeled "religion" and "spirituality," or "religion" and "New Age," with the second section usually much larger than the first. The New Age movement is the clearest specific example of "spirituality," but by no means is it the only one. "Spirituality" has seeped into many churches and private lives like gas from a leak in an underground pipe.

The conversation continued. "There's another thing I don't like about Lewis: he's a pessimist."

"About man, you mean? Calling us sinners?"

"That too. But I mean about the future. About history."

This was my second surprise, for Harry, like any effective trail guide, fisherman or boat owner, had to believe in Murphy's Law.

I countered, "But Lewis *attacked* pessimism. He also attacked optimism. He saw them as opposite forms of the same error of historicism, or historical determinism."

Harry could give and take the ism words, but he gave me a blank stare and said, stubbornly, "Well, I believe in the future."

"I see."

"You don't?"

"No. I believe in God. I think he's more reliable than 'the future.'"

"You believe in God but you don't believe in the future?" (This seemed to be a new thought to him.)

"Right. The future hasn't given me any promises or covenants lately, or sent any prophets or saviors."

"I'll bet you're down on celebrating the millennium too, right?" (It was the year 2000.)

"That depends."

"On what?"

"On *why* you're celebrating the millennium."

"What's *your* reason?"

"My reason is what it's the third millennium *of*."

"Of?"

"Yes. The year 2001 will begin the third millennium *of what?*"

"You tell me. I dunno."

"Jesus Christ."

"Hey, don't go cursing me out just because I didn't pass your little test!"

"I wasn't cursing. In my language system, Jesus Christ isn't a curse word; he's the Word of God."

"Oh. I guess we live in different language systems. And language shapes your world, so I guess we live in different worlds."

"Yes, we do. But we live in the same society. And it's dying."

"Dying? Why?" (Another new thought.)

"Because it's turned the name of its Savior into a curse word."

Harry was silent and angry. I was sorry for the anger but thought it a price worth paying for the silence.

There are three kinds of people in Western civilization and they are clearly distinguishable by the answer they give you if you ask them why we celebrated the third millennium. (1) Only a minority will mention Christ. It is, of course, the third millennium *anno domini*, but the media mind molders kept that secret under wraps. (2) The answer of the molders and their moldees to our question is more likely to be a slightly more articulate version of "Duhhh." I classify "believers in the future" like Harry into this second class. They are, I fear, the majority. (3) A third group—the materialists—will answer the question by pointing to the "evolutionary accident" of ten fingers (two thousand is a multiple of ten).

If our whole society consisted only of the first and third groups (the intelligent Christians and the intelligent materialists, the committed supernaturalists and the committed naturalists), then real debate might ensue, with the likely result of a stream of conversions. It is the muddled middle that is the devil's triumph: the "spiritual" people.

These "spiritual" people do not believe in Christianity (though most of them think they are Christians), nor do they believe in atheism or materialism; they believe in "spirituality." They think religion—any religion—is a good thing not because it is true but because it fosters morality. (But they tend to reduce morality to compassion or "tolerance"—the virtue Chesterton said is all that remains after a man has lost all his principles.) At the same time they think religion is a bad thing not because it is a lie but because it fosters "fanaticism." (They do not know that all saints and all lovers are fanatics.) They say they like "religion" but not "organized religion." They have never been serious Christians; they have never joined a concrete church with its messy, stubborn, unwieldy members like the animals on Noah's ark, therefore they do not realize that the phrase "organized religion" is an oxymoron.

Both the "spiritualists" (group two) and the secularists (group three) believe in the future. The "spiritualists" believe in it because of sentiment and vague optimism. The secularists believe in it because of their lord and savior, Science. Only the first group, the religious (religious Jews, Christians and Muslims) are the infidels who do not bow the knee to the god Tomorrow.

Both the spiritualists and the secularists also disbelieve in the devil. The spiritualists disbelieve because of sentiment and vague optimism or because belief in the devil is not "compassionate." The secularists disbelieve because their lord and savior, Science, cannot detect the devil with any of its approved instruments, such as test tubes, math, anchorpersons or professors.

I think we can distinguish at least five different reasons why the "spiritualists" disbelieve in the devil. Believing in the devil means believing in (1) supernatural evil, (2) moral evil, (3) spiritual evil, (4) personal evil and (5) evil itself. Every "spiritualist" denies at least one of these five.

1. Some "spiritualists" are naturalists. Thus they disbelieve in supernatural evil.

2. Some "spiritualists" are amoralists who do not believe in moral evil (sin), only physical evil (pain). Sometimes this is because they are determinists, who do not believe in free will. Sometimes it is because they have a phobia against guilt and therefore against moral law, because they do not know the

only One who saves us from guilt, as from sin.

3. Some "spiritualists" are truly Gnostics, who identify spirit with goodness and thus implicitly identify matter with evil (though they no longer say that, as the original Gnostics did). So to them, "spiritual evil" is an oxymoron.

4. Some "spiritualists" are Marxists, socialists or other political leftists who do not believe in personal evil, individual evil, but only in evil social and economic systems and institutions. (I wonder where they think these systems came from?)

5. Finally, and most desperately, some "spiritualists" are cockeyed optimists who do not believe in evil at all. (After all, the word sounds so *judgmental!*)

The most influential man who ever lived did not fit into any of these five categories, and therefore he was able to believe in the devil. In fact, he did not *believe in* the devil; he *knew* the devil quite personally, from direct experience and encounter. Even more, he had *created* the devil and seen him fall.

This man, incidentally, also refutes the secularists' fallacy about the millennium, the idea that the accident of numbers (ten fingers, one thousand years) determines historical meanings. The very concept of the millennium—that is, the dating of history by Christ, B.C. versus A.D.—shows that the opposite is true, that meaning determines numbers, that the biological "accident" of man having ten fingers has been pressed into the service of Jesus Christ.

What do the "spiritualists" miss in denying the devil? Obviously, truth, knowledge of objective fact. (Unless, of course, Jesus is a fool deluded by a myth.) But what else? What is the existential import of this truth? What difference does Satan make?

The most obvious answer is that the "spiritualists" miss drama, verve, passion. In this world the height of the mountain is measured by the depth of the valley. This is no justification of Satan, evil or war, of course, but it is an undeniable fact that we appreciate good only by contrast with evil. Without Satan there is no drama because without Satan there is no history. History's plot, from a human point of view, is "challenge and response" (to use Toynbee's formula); and without some challenge of the bad, there is no response of the good; and without the first inventor of the bad, there is no challenge of the bad. History, like individual life, is essentially the drama of warfare between good and evil. Time began in Genesis 1, but history began in Genesis 3.

Evil is not trivial, and therefore its first inventor cannot be trivial. Satan must be chuckling over the modern media stereotype of himself as a horned clown in a red tutu, or the alternative one—more abstract but just as toothless—that sees him as a mythic projection of human weaknesses. For no one really fears either a clown or an abstraction.

Christ took Satan very seriously (though not obsessively). If we do not, how can we say our minds are on line with the Lord? If we claim to have matured beyond belief in Satan, we claim to have matured beyond Christ. If we scorn the fear of Satan as foolish, we are calling Christ a fool, for he told us to fear him (Matthew 10:28). And if we think of Christ as in any way a fool, we are either denying the Incarnation, denying that Christ is God, or else saying that God is a fool. For if fear of Satan is foolish, and if Christ taught it, and if Christ is God, then God is foolish.

Christ commanded us to conclude the only prayer he ever gave us, the model prayer, with "Rescue us from the evil one"

(Matthew 6:13). The Greek word is a singular noun, not a plural or a participle, and it has a definite article. The proper translation is not just "evil" but "the evil one."

Perhaps the most stunning movie ever made, the one that left audiences in shocked silence, truly terrified and changed, was *The Exorcist*. The reason for this is that it was real. It was based on an actual exorcism case, carefully researched and written by William Peter Blatty, who actually believed in Satan. One of its scenes used a tape recording that had been made in an actual exorcism. The audience heard the actual voice of a demon. The difference between this and all other "demon movies" in its effect on audiences was a difference in kind, not degree. For audiences who watched the fictional *Exorcist* II, time and breath did not stop, flesh did not crawl and total silence did not descend.

The real devil is magnetically attractive. He comes to us not disguised as a buffoon but as "an angel of light" (2 Corinthians 11:14). He is more formidable than anything we have ever seen in this world, even the sea. "And he's very, very big!"—to quote a suggestive line from Ingmar Bergman's *The Seventh Seal*.

Luther's great hymn "A Mighty Fortress Is Our God" gets it just right: Satan is both formidable and doomed. We are ants to him, but he is an ant to Christ.

> For still our ancient Foe
> Doth seek to work us woe;
> His craft and power are great,
> And, armed with cruel hate,
> On earth is not his equal.
>
> Did we in our own strength confide,
> Our striving would be losing;

Were not the right Man on our side,
The Man of God's own choosing.
Dost ask who that may be?
Christ Jesus, it is he;
Lord Sabaoth his name,
From age to age the same,
And he must win the battle.

And though this world, with devils filled,
Should threaten to undo us;
We will not fear, for God has willed
His truth to triumph through us.
The Prince of Darkness grim,
We tremble not for him;
His rage we can endure,
For lo! his doom is sure;
One little word shall fell him.

That Word, above all earthly powers,
No thanks to them, abideth;
The Spirit and the gifts are ours
Through Him who with us sideth.
Let goods and kindred go,
This mortal life also;
The body they may kill;
God's truth abideth still;
His Kingdom is forever.

C. S. Lewis contends that we all unconsciously know the
real Satan:

The children, the poets, and the philosophers were right: as
there is one Face above all worlds merely to see which is irre-
vocable joy, so at the bottom of all worlds that face is waiting

whose sight alone is the misery from which none who beholds it can recover. And though there seemed to be, and indeed were, a thousand roads by which a man could walk through the world, there was not a single one which did not lead sooner or later to either the Beatific or the Miserific Vision. (*Perelandra*)

Satan apes God, for he is a liar and "the father of lies" (John 8:44). Michael the archangel exposes Satan's primordial lie with his very name: "Michael" means "Who is like God?" Satan pretends to be God's equal, God's opposite. This is a metaphysical impossibility, the greatest lie there is. Satan's equal, opposite and enemy is not God but Michael. But it is not us. Both Satan and Michael, both the demons and the angels, are far more formidable, more powerful and more intelligent than any human beings.

In the book of Revelation, Satan seduces man with his lie. He presents an unholy trinity to ape the Holy Trinity: "the Beast," "the Dragon" and "the false prophet." Furthermore, the "whore of Babylon" apes the "woman clothed with the sun," the unholy city Babylon apes the holy city Jerusalem and even the number 666—a trinity of sixes (six is the number of man)—aspires to the holy seven. Satan's time of triumph is also a seven broken in half, or "deconstructed," namely "a time, and [two] times, and half a time"—$1 + 2 + \frac{1}{2} = 3\frac{1}{2}$ (Revelation 12:14).

So it is no surprise that our reaction to the real Satan can ape our reaction to the real Christ in totally transcending *niceness*. The existential import of meeting Satan is much more like that of meeting Christ than like that of meeting our popular pictures of Satan. The real presence of Satan is shattering in its warlike hate, as the real presence of Christ is shattering in its peace and love. As Christ gives a peace the world cannot give, so Satan gives a war the world cannot give. As Christ offers a supernatural love, so Satan offers a supernatural hate. As Christ is a light that worldly darkness cannot comprehend and cannot overcome (John 1:5), so Satan is a darkness that worldly light cannot comprehend and cannot overcome.

Is the vision of Pope Leo XIII not the most reasonable hypothesis? What else explains the data? Just look at the twentieth century. It will surely be known forever as the century of genocide. Despite all its radically new inventions—computers, nuclear power, genetics, space travel—genocide is the one invention that most directly and radically changed the most lives (well over a hundred million), not from worse to better, or even from better to worse, but from alive to dead. Auschwitz, Hiroshima, the Gulag, Ukraine, Armenia, Rwanda, the killing fields of Pol Pot's Cambodia, Mao's Cultural Revolution, Sudan—what does this look like but the Marquis de Sade writ large? Many people today simply do not know about the incredible carnage. Many who know do not have concrete, pictorial knowledge but only abstract statistics. (Stalin said about the famine he engineered in the Ukraine, "One death is a tragedy; ten million is a statistic.") But no one who actually experienced any of these atrocities can believe that human nature alone was responsible for such unlimited and deliberate malice.

One chilling and telling sign that these evils came not from the finite realms of the world and the flesh but from the realm of the devil is the astonishing total absence, in every case, of anything like remorse in the perpetrators of these colossal evils. The demon, having done his work through his human instruments, then departs, and the killer feels no guilt, as if he had not been there, as if the deed had been done by someone else. For this is precisely what has happened. To have no remorse for having sliced apart pregnant women like meat, bayoneted babies like melons or systematically gassed six million Jews only because they were Jews is not human. Even the agnostic humanist, meeting such evil, approves the sentiment that this could not have been merely human. For if it were, the humanist would have to believe an even more pessimistic anthropology than that of the "original sin conservative" he despises.

As saints are filled with a more-than-human goodness, with a supernatural life, is it not equally obvious that the men who carried out these atrocities were filled with a more-than-human evil, a supernatural evil? As Paul said, "It is no longer I who live, but it is Christ who lives in me" (Galatians 2:20), so Hitler or Pol Pot could with equal truth have said, "It is no longer I who live, but it is Satan who lives in me." If supernatural goodness ever visited our world, it was two thousand years ago. (Even many humanists will approve this sentiment, though not the theology.) Equally, if supernatural evil ever visited our world, it was in the twentieth century. And not only in "primitive" places; the Holocaust happened in the heartland of Western civilization. And most Germans were not shocked.

But it is not over. Right here, right now, most Americans are much less shocked at the present abortion holocaust of the holy innocents than they are at the use of that biblical and Hebrew h-word to describe it. The *word* is more unacceptable than the *reality*! (The same is true of sodomy today: In many places that word is illegal "hate speech," but the reality is legal.) Is this not the deepest triumph of Satan? I mean the fact that we are not even mildly shocked at what our ancestors would have been utterly stunned by. Is this lack of shock in us not an even greater triumph of Satan than the things about which we are not shocked? Is he not even more pleased at killing consciences than killing bodies?

The horror of the century of genocide is behind us—or is it? It is continuing, but the awareness of it, the concern about it and the outrage against it are not. They are dying. Sometimes they are called "intolerance" or "hate speech."

The book of Revelation seems to suggest that Hitler was only a pale copy, a preliminary version, a trial run for the Antichrist. If we take seriously the only divinely authorized book of prophecy we have for our future, we find that history is destined to climax not in utopia and enlightenment and peace but in dystopia and darkness and war—in fact, in a paroxysm of evil called "the great tribulation" that, we are warned, is so unimaginably terrible that "if those days had not been cut short, no one would be saved." This is not the raving of a fundamentalist flake but our Lord's own words (Matthew 24:21-22).

On the other hand, if the twentieth century was the devil's chosen century, then the twenty-first is not, and therefore it must, it seems, be an improvement. Pope John Paul II, one of the most serious and realistic men of our time, is always hopeful, especially for youth and the coming generation. A repentance, a revival, a return, a second spring could happen—one that would make the twenty-first century the greatest in history.

No one but God knows which of these roads our culture will take. But we can know where the roads are; we can know the basic cultural road map. And that is our next point.

4

THE FUNDAMENTAL
PRINCIPLE OF ALL
CULTURE WARS

COLSON'S LAW

T he fourth thing we need to know to win the culture war is the fundamental law of all culture wars. I call it Colson's Law because I learned it from Chuck Colson, though I've forgotten the chapter and verse.

It is one of the most fundamental laws of human history. It has always been true, and it always will be true, unless human nature itself changes in its essence.

It could also be called the Law of Four C's: community, chaos, conscience and cops. It can be remembered best visually, like the square of opposition in logic:

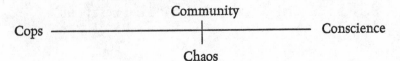

Community and chaos are "vertical" opposites of good versus evil, while cops and conscience are "horizontal" opposites of two goods. Community and chaos are inherently opposed forces, like battling armies. Cops and conscience are the two possible weapons or strategies of the defensive army (community) against the offensive army (chaos). Both pairs of opposites are inversely proportionate, but the "vertical" opposites are necessarily opposed (chaos and community destroy each other), while the horizontal are not. In fact, cops and conscience are often complementary. But the *need* for each one decreases as the supply of the other one increases: the more conscience a community has, the fewer cops it needs; and the more cops it has, the less conscience it needs to rely on.

Chaos is to a community what disease is to a body. (For the body politic is also a body; its unity is organic rather than artificial.) Community integrates; chaos disintegrates. Community is coinherence; chaos is incoherence. Community is construction; chaos is deconstruction. (A whole philosophy today proudly names itself after this process.)

A community is an organic unity because it is a microcosm, a little picture of the universe itself. Though God created the universe from without, he designed it to be held together from within, "naturally," by its own inner force of unity, not propped up by external force. Like a human community, the "universe" is the paradox of a one ("uni") in many ("versa") or many in one. Like the universe, a "community" is the paradox of a "common unity" of many individuals and subgroups united in a common work, for a common purpose and sharing a common value.

Augustine defined the unifying soul of a community (*civitas*, "city") as a common love. Thus there are ultimately only two "cities," the City of God (God-lovers) and the City of the World (world-worshipers, idolaters). A community as well as an individual can truly claim Augustine's beautiful formula "*amor meus, pondus meum*"—my love is my weight, my gravity, my destiny. My *density* is my *destiny*. (Remember that seren-dipitous malapropism of George McFly's pick-up line in *Back to the Future*?)

Let's look at our social body by analogy with our individual body. The human body has two shields against disease: inner and outer, natural and artificial, preventive and remedial. If it loses its inner immunity to disease, it needs medicines, sur-gery or crutches to prop it up from the outside, to compensate for its inner disintegration. Cripples need crutches for the same reason sinners need churches. Religion is indeed a crutch, a defensive weapon, a shield.

And social bodies as well as individual bodes need shields. Like the body physical, the body politic has two shields against chaos: the outer shield is "positive law," that is, human law, which is enforced physically by cops. The inner shield is "natural law," moral law not *made* by man but *discovered*, which is enforced spiritually by conscience.

The inner shield is made of freedom; the outer shield is made of force. The inner shield is love—love of the good. The outer shield is fear—the fear of punishment. And love is free, while fear is unfree.

Colson's Law dictates that a community with fewer "inner cops" needs more "outer cops." America's Founding Fathers saw this and repudiated an unfree state based primarily on "outer cops." They explicitly said that the free democracy they were designing was designed *only* for a moral people. The foundation stones for a democracy are consciences.

But the paradox of democracy is that it is founded on the premise of strong moral consciences yet tends to produce weak ones by its very permissiveness. Its maximization of freedom (that is, freedom from cops) depends on its willing submission to conscience, yet this freedom from cops tempts us to free ourselves from conscience too. And then, paradoxically, this excess of external, physical freedom requires more cops to stave off internal, spiritual chaos (which erupts into external public chaos sooner or later). Thus we get more cops and *less* freedom. For the two kinds of freedom—from conscience and from cops—are also inversely proportionate. The more of either one you have, the less you need the other. (Think this through!)

Colson's Law states that the only alternatives to conscience are cops or chaos. If the inner shield is lowered, the outer shield must be raised to prevent chaos. Therefore, a democracy that loses its conscience will necessarily become a totalitarianism.

The point should be obvious, but it sounds shocking to most Americans. And that fact itself is shocking.

The idea of America becoming totalitarian will seem absurd to most Americans, but that is because they forget that there is what de Tocqueville called a "soft totalitarianism" as well as a "hard totalitarianism," a *Brave New World* as well as a *1984*. The dictatorship of what Rousseau called "the general will," that is, popular opinion, can be just as totalitarian as that of any king or tyrant, and much harder to topple, especially when manipulated by a powerful and ideologically united media. For the media are more powerful than the military; the pen is indeed mightier than the sword.

The cops in a "soft totalitarianism" wield pens rather than

swords—for example, speech codes that see "hate speech," "right-wing extremism" and "homophobia" in more places than medieval inquisitors saw devils and witches.

Colson's Law is based on observation of history. It is not ideological, and therefore it does not presuppose either conservatism or liberalism. Liberals and conservatives differ only about the accidents of Colson's Law, not the essence. There are very significant differences between liberals and conservatives, of course. Liberals trust cops less than conservatives do. And much more importantly, liberals today usually think conscience comes from society, not from God or from human nature and the "natural law." But they agree with conservatives that conscience is better than cops at preserving community from chaos, so they too usually agree that society needs moral education. Thus a new coalition of liberals and conservatives may be arising that wants to teach values and even virtues.

For liberals as well as conservatives agree with Colson's Law. I think the deepest reason for this hopeful phenomenon is that both liberals and conservatives, being humans, have a common experience, which includes raising children—and *everyone* tries to apply Colson's Law in raising their children. They try to teach children to substitute internal controls for external controls, to internalize the restraints against chaos that began as external, parental and societal authority—in other words, to replace cops with conscience. A practical social alliance is thus possible and necessary. The left and right wings can beat together, and the sick bird can fly again. The ill eagle does not have to be immoral.

Colson's Law is science rather than sermon, empirical rather than ideological. We can see the law at work in the history of any body, individual or collective, and we can make predictions on the basis of this law. Any individual human body that loses its immune system will die unless it is propped up by many artificial, external aids: pills, operations, prosthetics. And even then, it's only a matter of time until it dies. The same is true of social bodies: police states without consciences are brittle. The "Thousand-Year Reich" lasted twelve years. The longest-lasting societies in history were all highly moralistic, including the Confucian (over twenty-one hundred years), the Islamic (almost fourteen hundred years) and the Roman (about seven hundred years). The longest-lasting moral order in history was that of Mosaic law: it has structured Jewish and then Christian life for thirty-five hundred years (though not as a continuous civil society).

Confucian society, which held together the world's largest nation for the world's longest time, was toppled from without by history's greatest mass murderer: Mao Zedong. Rome began as a moralistic republic and evolved into an amoral empire that became a totalitarian police state and fell from within. Islamic society is still growing, especially in Christian places. Christianity is still growing everywhere except in Christian places, and especially in anti-Christian places like Sudan and China. Persecution multiplies Christians like stomping on a ball of mercury.

Colson's Law predicts that a community's longevity is proportionate to its morality.

And to its religion, for no society has yet existed that has successfully built its knowledge of morality on any basis other than religion. In theory the natural moral law can be known by natural human reason alone without knowing the supernaturally revealed divine law, but in practice this is very rare; there has never been a whole society of Platos and Aristotles. It is a massive and obvious fact of history that religion has always been the primary source of mankind's knowledge of morality. This fact is so obvious that no age ever ignored it except this one.

Even if explicit religion is not the source of morality's *being*, it has certainly been the source of morality's being *known and taught*. No officially secular society has yet survived more than seventy-two years, the U.S.S.R. being history's clearest test case. If the results of *that* test are not clear, nothing in history is.

The West has been the body that has carried the Mosaic law so far. Other social bodies, of course, could carry this moral and religious heritage. Judaism was "moved" from Israel in A.D. 70, and it was not moved back again until 1948. The Church moved from Jerusalem to Antioch and then to Rome as its center. It could move again, if necessary, as a family moves from a decaying neighborhood into a new house. It may have to do so if things do not change.

For Western civilization seems to have contracted moral AIDS. America, though only 225 years old, is already in crisis, like a child with progeria (premature aging). Eventual death is inevitable for any body, of course (except a supernatural one); but the decay of a body's immune system, whether physical or spiritual, means not just dying but dying young and dying in pain.

Diseases of the spirit as well as the body can be cured—but only if they are diagnosed. Where did we catch this disease? And where is it coming from now? Find the cause and you may be able to find the cure.

We seem to have caught the disease during the ironically named "Enlightenment," which closed our eyes to God and had the chutzpah to pin the label "Dark Ages" on the Age of Light, that is, the Age of Faith. This linguistic irony is not surprising, for language is one of a dying society's first organs to be infected, as Confucius clearly saw. Asked to name the single most important one of his many social principles of reform, he answered, "The restoration of language," calling things by their proper names.

The irony continues when we seek the *ongoing* source of the disease, for the disease is coming mainly from the doctors, the "experts," the social specialists. There is a terrible double irony here: just as 99 percent of the violent murders in America are committed legally by healers who have become hypocritic instead of Hippocratic, so the main source of the murder of morality is our moralists, our mind molders, our educators, both formal (in schools and universities) and informal (in media). And they in turn have been trained by our prophets and high priests, our psychologists and sociologists, who are the most irreligious and relativistic segment in our society. (One sociologist, Peter Berger, called America "a nation of Indians ruled by an elite of Swedes," since India is the most religious nation in the world and Sweden is the least.)

Together our mind-molding media constitute a nonorganized religion of missionaries who are evangelizing religious people out of their primitive superstitions like poverty, chastity and obedience and into the missionaries' new, "enlightened" religion of greed, lust and pride (that is, money, sex and power); out of peace with neighbor, self and God and into peace with the world, the flesh and the devil.

Treatment of a disease is always most effective if it is applied to the source of the disease itself, rather than somewhere else, later and further down the line of dominoes that the disease has already knocked down. In other words, to cure this social disease we must infiltrate its social sources. To put it clearly and bluntly, we must infiltrate the psychology and sociology departments, along with the popular journalism and media production centers, that is, the mind-molding areas of the battlefield. The most powerful forces in America are no longer church and state bu Harvard and Hollywood. Church and state have limited power, for we are free to ignore or leave any church, and we are free to vote out of office any politician. But we are not free to stop our ears to the educational and media blitz that assaults us everywhere, the buzzing flies of Beelzebub that hover around the garbage dumps of the minds that make the movies and TV shows. It is on these screens that we find the flies, and it is on these screens that we must apply the swatters.

Who are the fly swatters? Not censors but saints. Love makes more waves than hate. Wicked men will hate and fear you more for loving them than for hating them. They will quickly forgive you for being wrong, but they will never forgive you for being right.

Saints always go into the ghettos, especially the moral ghettos. They make waves. Moses made waves. Jesus made waves. Muhammad made waves. The waves make the garbage come to the surface, and the waves of garbage often drown the saints and make them martyrs, white corpuscles that give themselves up to fight an infection. Saints are society's white corpuscles, society's saviors. If nobody wants to crucify you, you're not doing your job. Or else your job isn't *his* work.

5

OUR ENEMY'S BATTLE PLAN

SATAN'S STRATEGY FOR THE THIRD MILLENNIUM

I will not tell you how this speech fell into my hands.

It was apparently written by Satan himself, and his listeners to it are demons: a captive audience. Please keep in mind when reading this speech that its author is the father of lies, and therefore nearly everything he says is a half-truth.

*   *   *

My deliciously dear, damnably darling demidevils! I announce to you good news (that is, bad news, of course: with us, "fair is foul and foul is fair"). We may stand at a Gettysburg-like turning point in the Great War, the only war there is, the (please excuse the obscene M-word) Mother of all wars. We may be in a position to inflict on our ancient Enemy's body on earth a wound so grievous that it will issue in the Great Tribulation and the Last Days, the final phase of our triumph.

To understand this, we need to review our grand strategy: its past, its present and its future.

To begin at the beginning: I am personally opposed to absolutes, or ultimates, so I will not speak of our ultimate origin. Our enemies keep circulating the ridiculous rumor that we were created by the Enemy. How utterly unendurable *that* would be!

Nor will I speak of our ultimate end. Our enemies have popularized the myth of some unthinkable final defeat of ours. What nonsense!

But I *will* speak of the present. Well, actually the real present is to be avoided too, like the ultimate past and the ultimate future. But I will speak of the specious present, the abstract present, the vague present, the pseudohistorical present, the present climate of opinion, the modern mind, the Zeitgeist, the current fashion among the media elite, the consensus of contemporary experts—which to us is like waves to surfers.

But to assess the present moment and our future prospects, a few remarks about the historical past are in order. Here is hell's brief history of time.

Ever since I began our great war by asserting my rights, my freedom and my self-actualization against the narrow-minded, bigoted, tyrannical, Fascistic, chauvinistic, racist, sexist, homophobic dogmatism and right-wing fundamentalist fanaticism of the Enemy; ever since I proclaimed the profound philosophical principle of absolute relativism and persuaded you to follow this super-enlightened program of revolutionary political correctness, we have won victory after

victory. Conclusively and repeatedly have we demons demon-
strated that straight is stupid and crooked is clever.

Of course there was that little temporary setback when we
were forcibly ejected from heaven. But that is more than com-
pensated for by our assurance that our triumph is guaranteed. (I
promise you total customer satisfaction or double your money
back.) For the very essence of heaven's philosophy is weakness,
and the very essence of hell's philosophy is strength and power.
Heaven relies on love (gag! choke! spit!)—pardon the obscen-
ity—while hell relies on fear. (Let's hear your cheer for fear!
Hear, hear!) And as our beloved prophet Mack the Knife Yav-
elli pointed out so irrefutably in The Prince, "It is better to be
feared than to be loved, for men will love you as *they* choose, but
they will fear you as *you* choose."

Because of this weakness of the Enemy, that is, because of
his obsession with love (cough! gag! vomit!), he has handed us
our victory. For though we cannot storm his fortress heaven,
we can corrupt his beloved colony earth. We cannot harm
him, but we *can* harm—heh! heh!—we can *eternally* harm—
those stupid talking animals he loves so obsessively. Love has
made him hostage to *their* happiness.

This weakness of love is so obvious that it is incredible that
he has not admitted it by now and abandoned his failed philosophy. For love multiplies your sorrows and your defeats by
the number of others you love and by the depth of your love
for each one. Of course his saints keep claiming that love also
multiplies your joys by the same two multipliers—but this is
simply nonsense. What *is* "joy," anyway? What does it mean?
Not one of us has ever found any intelligible content to this
empty myth, this meaningless mantra mumbled by the
Enemy's troops.

Thus, because of the Enemy's love addiction, we have been able to conquer him millions of times in conquering his creatures, whom he lowers himself to call his "children." (Imagine the indignity: the one who claims to be the creator of angels stoops to be the father of talking animals only slightly superior to slime and slugs!) How wise I was to foresee the inevitable failure of love and to attack at the very beginning, when there were only two of these creatures to corrupt. Because of the Enemy's obscene invention of breeding and heredity, I thus assured that all their descendants would be born with their newly corrupted nature, doomed to death. (Yes, to death! Here's to death! Let's drink to death, my demidevils!)

They cannot now imagine the enormity of the gap between what they are now and what they were then, before our glorious victory in Eden, because their very minds are corrupted and darkened and addicted to appearances (which did not change much) instead of intuiting invisible essences, including their own, which changed radically. But we can clearly behold the measure of our success: the Grand Canyon, the gap between eating unforbidden fruit, playing with tame animals and making love in Eden and eating the fruit of our lies, playing with untamed animal passions and making war east of Eden!

How easy it is to kill, how hard to heal! How easily Cain killed Abel! How hard was Cain's rock; how soft was Abel's head! How weak and defenseless is the unborn baby against the abortionist's vacuum tubes and bone crushers! And how weak is the conscience of its parents against our propaganda! So legal, so respectable, so *proper* it seems to a human—the silly goose! Well, we've found the perfect mate for a proper goose: a propaganda.

There is one question our Central Intelligence Agency has never been able to answer: How could the Enemy ignore such a truism? How can one who seemed to us once to be so super-intelligent, even omniscient, possibly be so super-stupid as to ignore the truism that a cage of lions are sufficient to eat a coliseum of Christians; that one bull can ruin a whole china shop, one affair a whole marriage, one mass murderer a whole classroom of schoolchildren?

And once evil begins, it cannot end. It is immortal—as immortal as we are, as immortal as our very being, now that we have identified our very being with evil. There can be no victory over evil. For the very laws of logic decree that one can make only two responses to evil: yes or no. If they say yes to evil, they condone it. If they say no, they condemn it. But then we easily turn them into condemners, haters, naysayers, witch-hunters and inquisitors.

They say they have a solution to our dilemma of yes or no with this other meaningless thing they call "forgiveness." This simply doesn't work, for two reasons. First, because they usually think this means the forgiveness of *sins* instead of the forgiveness of *sinners*; but that's simply condoning. Second, because even if they do understand this, they simply can't practice the distinction they preach, separating sins from sinners. So they either hate both, hate sinners along with sins (and that was our primary temptation to them in the past), or else they love both, love sins along with sinners (and this is our primary temptation to them in the present). They find it extremely difficult to burn heresies without burning heretics, or to accept heretics without accepting heresies. The only solution they've come up with so far was the suggestion of a religious rock group called Cool Inquisition: to solve the heresy problem compassionately by cryogenics: *freezing* heretics instead of burning them, and thawing them out at the end of the world. You see what ludicrous lengths we've driven them to even in their feeble attempts at humor.

Even when our success was evident, the Enemy would not admit his mistake. Like the general who ordered the charge of the light brigade, he kept sending prophet after prophet into the battle—and we kept mopping up the prophets. Many a human CEO wonders what eats up his profits, but the CEO of the universe knows very well what eats up *his* prophets: us. (Yum, yum!)

And then he made his supreme mistake, the culmination of love's folly. He must have reasoned, "They did not spare my prophets, but surely they will spare my Son. Surely they are not so wicked as that. Surely Satan has not succeeded that spectacularly in putting out the fires of my love in their hearts. Surely evil is not stronger than divine love incarnate."

The Incarnation seemed to be his great triumph, his D-Day. But I outwitted him, there in the wilderness, when I tempted his Son with the whole world if only he would fall down and worship me. You see, I there presented him with a dilemma that was logically impossible for him to escape. For I hold millions of his beloved children hostage in hell eternally. I offered to release them all to him, empty hell itself, give him the whole world—that is, the world of human souls—if only he would worship me instead of his Father. If he did it, I would split the eternal Trinity. The Son's will would deviate from the Father's. If not, I would keep millions of his beloved children forever.

He refused to split the Trinity's will, but I got to split the

Trinity anyway, on the cross. If I could not introduce division into eternal Oneness by splitting the Trinity's *will*, then I would split the Trinity's *happiness*, the Enemy's very presence to himself! That's what I achieved at Golgotha, the place of the triumph of death, the Place of the Skull. I spilled his blood and his happiness; I introduced death into divinity, death into the heart of life! "*Eli, Eli, lama sabachthani*"—"My God, my God, why hast thou forsaken me?" Ahhhh, I can still taste it: the ecstasy of evil, the triumph over the so-called Lord himself! The taste of that triumph will never leave the mouth of my memory. I will gnaw on that bone forever.

How could we ever have respected that divine fool when we lived in heaven? He would not call down the twelve legions of angels to do battle for him even then—the putrid, pablum-eating pacifist! He even forbade Peter's war against the high priest's servant's right ear, the justest war in human history. Right into my trap he stepped, right into the hands of *my* people: Judas, Caiaphas, Herod, Caesar, Pilate.

Ooooh, love that Pilate! What a politician! "Shall we crucify him?" "Well, I'm personally opposed, but . . ." How we lead them around by their buts! Every hour around the world for thousands of years *his* name has been mouthed millions of times as Christians say their creed: "suffered under Pontius Pilate." And how many "personally opposed" Pilates have we cloned today in how many congresses? And in how many universities whose professors profess nothing but professionalism, whose only truth is Pilate's other wonderfully slimy saying: "Truth? Schmooth!" or something like that.

And just look at the mileage we got out of our other friend, Judas Iscariot, the first Christian to accept a government grant. We've gotten *his* disciples to take much more than thirty pieces of silver today. And still our Enemy keeps back his angels!

Of course there was that sneaky little trick of the resurrection that he pulled off. That may well have cost us the war, had he not reverted to his old, failed policy of "hands off" afterward, ascended back into heaven and left his children in the hands of baby-sitters like John XXII, Torquemada, Richelieu and more recently, in the hands of sponges like Bishop Spong at one end of the seesaw and swaggerers like Jimmy Swaggart at the other.

You see, my hearties? He's still the fool. We still rule the world. I am still the prince of the power of the air—of ABC and NBC and CBS, my unholy trinity. Just look at what became of his grand plan for "redemption." Just look at what he accomplished by walking into my jaws of death on the cross. Just look at the world today. If *that's* a world redeemed, I'm a horny toad.

And just look at the century that just ended, our favorite century. There is a rumor going around that long ago the Enemy offered me one century for me to do my worst work in, and I chose the twentieth. Hah! As if I had to beg scraps from *his* table! What really happened was that I told *him* what century I would take, and he backed down and let me have it.

At the beginning of the twentieth century some omniverously obtuse optimists founded a journal with the purportedly prophetic title of The *Christian Century*. Due to the success of our historical grand strategy, we can be quite sure that the one title future historians will *not* use for the twentieth century is *that* one.

There remains, of course, that bothersome little matter of the Enemy's Church, that ratty little band of invaders in *our* world, with its infuriatingly tenacious little beachhead. For the first thousand years after the Enemy's invasion planted its seeds, we could not stop its growth. But then we learned a few elementary military principles, and they have brought us to our present pinnacle of success. I will now review five of these principles.

First, we learned to use the very success of the Enemy's forces to bring about their failure. Once we stopped indulging our appetite for martyr's blood and instead deliberately let the Church get big and fat and comfortable and successful, we found that its very strength became its weakness. We lost the first millennium because the blood of the martyrs was the seed of the Church, but we won the second millennium because the power of the princes was the dryrot of the Church.

Whenever these humans get power, they get corruption. Power corrupts. It just does! Isn't it wonderful?

What happened in ancient Israel happened again to the Church in the second millennium. Review that spiritual graph of the history of the Church some time, down in the War Room, and compare it to the one for the history of Israel. If you don't see the common shape, back you go to boot camp! Every time the line rises, through repentance and obedience to the Enemy, and then consequent blessings, it turns to luxury and pride, and then of course it falls into destruction and misery. Next, alas, the misery prods them to repentance again, and the cycle begins over. You may think we cannot win because every time we are successful in corrupting their success, the cycle turns up again. But equally, every time the Enemy is successful, we corrupt *his* success and the cycle turns down again. We have achieved a perpetual standoff, a draw, a stalemate. We are as indestructible as the Enemy.

And that is *our* success, not his. For he claims to be stronger and to be able to destroy evil forever. The cycle shows that he is the father of lies and the father of follies. A draw is a win for us and our philosophy that good and evil are equal.

Throughout the twentieth century, we used this cycle principle successfully. Unfortunately, so has the Enemy. Look at China. China opened its doors to the Enemy's missionaries from the West at the beginning of the century. The Church had it easy there. By the fifties, there were 2 million converts out of a billion Chinese. Then we let our wild dog loose. Mao Zedong slaughtered more people than any butcher in history—about 50 million—and especially targeted the Enemy's people. And then, after Mao died and the doors opened again, the West discovered that there were not 2 million but almost 50 million of the Enemy's people in China. Persecution had multiplied them almost twenty-five times in fifty years.

Look at Poland. Under Communism, they all went to church and refused to take down their crucifixes from their public school classrooms even when state soldiers threatened them. And now that Poland is free, what do they all want? Abortions! What did East Germans look for in West Germany when the Berlin Wall came down? Porn shops!

Look at America. Ninety percent Christian, 50 percent churchgoers and one of the most selfish, self-indulgent and violent societies on earth. Their favorite word is "freedom," not "virtue," and their favorite song is the one everyone sings when they arrive in hell: "I Did It My Way." Now there's a triumph truer than Mao's. Our pleasure in contemplating this success is more subtle than our orgies of enjoyment of martyrs' pains, but it is more lasting and profitable in the long run. We are learning to prefer it, learning to be spiritual gourmets.

Here is a second principle of our successful strategy in the second millennium, a second way of dealing with that stupid little beachhead the Enemy still hangs on to by the skin of his teeth...

*   *   *

I cannot help interrupting and interjecting here that we must constantly remember that Satan is a propagandist and a master of slanting. Christianity, which he calls a "stupid little beachhead the Enemy still hangs on to by the skin of his teeth" now numbers about two billion souls out of six billion globally—by far the world's largest religion. If you add philosophical theists, religious Jews and Muslims (who now number about a billion), one out of every two people on earth worships the God of Abraham. That's calling half the world a "little beachhead."

*   *   *

Our second principle is the most elementary in all military strategy: divide and conquer. We finally realized how simple it was, after a thousand years of failure: we split the Enemy's Church in two in 1054. But the most successful attack was in 1517. That produced not two but over twenty thousand different denominations.

This second principle, divide and conquer, has produced the same successful result as the first principle, the corruptibility of power. That result is the persistence of evil. Evil cannot be undone! For evil divides and destroys, and it is always easier to divide than to unite, easier to destroy than to create.

It takes only one little push to knock Humpty-Dumpty off the wall, but once he is down on the ground and broken into many pieces, not all the king's horses nor all the king's men can put Humpty-Dumpty back together again. The Church can no more be reunited than an egg can be unscrambled.

Many hope that the third millennium may be the millennium of Christian reunification as the first was the millennium of Christian unity and the second was the millennium of Christian disunity. But this *must* be a bravado born of desperation. For we know this is impossible. Logic forbids it. For the different churches contradict each other, and two contradictions cannot both be true, and unity between the true and the false cannot be true unity. All they can do is compromise, and that is to weaken themselves even more. They have been struggling with the problem of "comparative religions" for a century now, and the only result is that they have become comparatively religious.

Even if they stop hating each other, even if their hearts reunite, their heads can't. Their divisions are eternal. In fact, they are doomed to divide forever, until eventually there are as many Christian churches as there are Christians. And *that's* the religion where the more sincere you are, the fewer converts you make: the worship of yourself.

No army can win battles when it's fighting civil wars against itself. But they can't stop those civil wars without compromise and indifference. Thus our victory is assured. Divisions are as irreversible as the cycles of history. Our second principle is as secure and as successful as our first.

But it gets even better. The division *between* churches is only one of three great divisions we've fomented. A second is the division *within* each church between the faithful and the "dissenters." (Back when they still believed in truth, they called them "heretics." People who call moral laws "values" call heretics "dissenters.") In the past these rebels would leave the Church and attack her from without, usually quite ineffectively. Now most of them stay, as spies, and attack her from within, much more effectively.

And there's a third division. We have set their two absolutes against each other: truth and love, justice and compassion. We have divided their hearts from their heads, flesh from bone, soft from hard. And we did that by politicizing their religion into Left versus Right, or liberal versus conservative. What they call "the Left" now means a heart without a head, and what they call "the Right" means a head without a heart. Their so-called conservatives go into orbit when liberals use the word *compassion*, and their so-called liberals suffer apoplexy when conservatives use the word *truth*.

They once tried to put themselves back together again by trying a mutual heart and brain transplant between a liberal and a conservative, but it didn't work for two reasons: they couldn't find any conservative who was willing to give his heart to a liberal, and they couldn't find any liberal who had any brains left to give, since they were so open-minded that their brains had spilled out.

In the past, we religionized their politics, and that got us some nice mileage, like persecutions and religious wars. But our current policy of politicizing their religion is proving even more successful. We've gotten most of them to classify themselves as liberal or conservative and then use these political categories to classify their faith, instead of vice versa. They now use the world's categories to judge the Church instead of using the Church's categories to judge the world.

They were supposed to judge *angels*, according to the Enemy's Scriptures. Ha! They're so nonjudgmental now that they won't even judge *sins*. The only thing they'll judge is judgmentalism. What fun we immortals have with what fools these mortals be!

For instance, take their "feminists." (Oh, please do!) They demand ordination to the priesthood—guess why? For "empowerment." I kid you not. That's what they say. I wonder when they'll start demanding martyrdom for "empowerment." What a great propaganda triumph for our Linguistic Obfuscation Department to get them to call those Amazons "feminists"!

Time for our third principle: the Big Lie.

You've got to get them educated before they'll fall for the Big Lie. They still see through all sorts of little lies, but the bigger it is, the harder they fall for it. The more educated they are, the more they think of themselves as radicals and bold nonconformists even as they're following each other around a circle like sheep, nose to tail. Well, we've gotten the bloody little bleaters to fall for the very essence of hell's philosophy: absolute relativism.

This was the philosophy behind *my* original glorious rebellion against the Enemy, when I refused to let *him* define reality or truth or goodness for *me*. I am who I am; I am the measure of all things—of what is real, of what is true and of what is good; of the origin, of the meaning and of the end; of the creation of being, of the design of being and of the appreciation of being; of the Father, and of the Son and of the Holy Spirit.

We have taught them this philosophy so well that they now demand not only autonomy, independence and "self-actualization" but even the right to define for oneself the meaning of the mystery of existence. Whew! Even Prometheus didn't go that far. But those are the words of their great legal philosopher Judas—I mean Justice—Anthony Kennedy, writing for their Supreme Court in the "Casey at the Bat" decision. The Supreme Court has now elevated this into a fundamental legal right in order to justify that other "right" they've demanded and practiced for a generation now: the right to murder their own unborn sons and daughters. (Bravo, Baal! Magnificent, Moloch! Awesome, Ashtoreth!)

Once we get them to believe in relativism and subjectivism, and to disbelieve in objective truth, it doesn't matter what else they believe or disbelieve. Even if they believe in the Enemy and his Son and his Spirit and his Church and his Law, as long as it's only on the basis of their own minds, we have won. For that basis is in *our* slimy little manipulating hands. And we can make it move wherever *our* fingers point. Once we control the premise, we control the conclusion.

On the other hand, if we don't control the premise, we don't control the conclusion. Even an adamant atheist who believes in objective truth is not securely in our clutches. He has the Enemy's premise (objective truth) even though he has our conclusion (atheism) for a while. We have to keep at him constantly to keep him from seeing the many paths that lead from the Enemy's premise to the Enemy's conclusion. Indeed, the Enemy's Son spoke the truth when he said, "Search, and you will find." So our essential task is not just to block the finding but to block the seeking; not just to get them off right roads and onto wrong roads for a while, but to get them to throw away all their road maps, their principles, their belief in objective truth, especially about good and evil.

Now their masses have not yet been massively suckered. You still can't fool a farmer half as easily as you can fool a scholar. But at the beginning of the century there were ten farmers for every scholar; now there are ten scholars for every farmer. The teachers buy our lies much more tamely than the students—and soon they'll all be teachers!

(Actually, one study estimated an even more apocalyptic future: that in two generations, at the present rate of growth, every single American citizen will be a lawyer! Need I say more? What's that? No, no, not *Thomas* More, you idiots!— he's the lawyer who got away.)

The three main sets of teachers in their society today, the three main mind-molding establishments, are formal education, informal education (that is, entertainment) and journalism. (They call these last two the "media.") All three are eating out of our claws. See why it's working? Once you get the teachers, you soon get the students. What's important is not the effect but the cause, not the conclusion but the premise, not the students but the teachers.

It's working. They let Moloch back, in a three-piece suit. Canaanites and Carthaginians and Aztecs now write the school textbooks and TV scripts. Only 3 percent of media mind molders say they support any limitations at all on the latest fashion in human sacrifice (abortion), while 80 percent of the public do. The teachers are far more advanced than the students. One study showed that German soldiers' willingness to participate in Hitler's holocaust—not just to approve it but to perform actual torture on prisoners—was directly proportionate to their level of education. In America it's the same: approval of *their* holocaust is directly proportionate to how much education they've had. In our schools, of course. The joke is that they still think they're *their* schools. And they keep their kids in because they're more concerned about saving their society's schools than about saving their children's souls.

The Enemy's people think they are safe from us because we cannot create or move matter, as the Enemy can, but all we can do is tempt and influence thought. Ha! "All we can do" is quite enough. For as one of their poets sagely said, "Sow a thought, reap an act; sow an act, reap a habit; sow a habit, reap a character; sow a character, reap a destiny." Their thoughts are their premises; their lives—and their eternal lives—are their conclusions. Get those premises! Occupy the premises! Conquer their philosophy. That strategy works especially well in American society because they don't pay much attention to philosophy, so they let their guard down there.

In fact, we have been able to smuggle the finest, most advanced form of sophism in human history into their universities as their most avant-garde, politically correct philosophy: deconstructionism, which has the chutzpah to say that truth itself is nothing but the hypocritical mask on the face of power. Oh, bravo! An A-plus for that one. I couldn't have put it better myself. Exactly the epistemology of hell. We usually have to tolerate a little truth before we twist it, but this bunkum is pure. We had to tolerate a few virtues even in our old heroes of hatred like Hitler before we could twist them—like patriotism and courage and passion. We had to let our old nihilistic existentialists like Sartre and Nietzsche and Beckett and Camus at least rise to the dignity of despair. But the philosophy of these new slimy snakes is a pure sneer, disguised by the cleverest linguistic tricks. Oooh, I love it! Imitation: the sincerest form of flattery.

Keep it up. And don't appeal to reason, even fallacious reason. The worst thing we could do now would be to try to rework the old kind of sophism, the appeal to fallacious reason. Fallacious is fine, but reason is dangerous. Behind all the old sophistries we used to tempt them to were three dangerous things: their attention to reason, their attention to truth and their attention to the issues. Three dangerous premises, and even though we put fallacies like banana peels on the paths between those premises and their conclusions, some of them found their way through without slipping. Eventually, seekers find. So it is a vastly more efficient expenditure of energy to attack the seeking, not the finding; the premises, not the conclusions; reason itself, not specific arguments.

One overconfident tempter—a bright-eyed and bushy-tailed beginner named Braintwister—recently tempted a philosophy professor to publish an ontological argument for the nonexistence of the devil (as if we needed them to doubt my existence any more). It was a mirror image of St. Anselm's famous ontological argument for the existence of the Enemy. It went like this. Anselm's argument had said that if the Enemy by definition is the most perfect conceivable being, who must have all conceivable perfections by definition; and that if real, objective existence is one conceivable perfection; then the Enemy must exist. So the professor argued that the same principle proves the *nonexistence* of the *least* perfect conceivable being: me. (Thank you, thank you! Don't clap; just throw souls.)

A wholly ungood being with the one perfection of real existence would not be wholly ungood—not as wholly ungood as one without even that one little perfection. Therefore I do not exist. Very clever indeed. But quite apart from the fact that the two fallacies in Anselm's argument are already exposed (ever since Augustine distinguished between moral perfection and ontological perfection and Kant noticed that "existence is not a predicate"), Braintwister's mistake was to feed the dangerous human interest in reasoning, their curiosity about truth and their wonder about whether I really exist or not. So Braintwister gave away three farms to buy one pig in a poke.

You tasted his fate last night at the banquet: that was Braintwister sauce flavoring those tepid souls we dined on. Let his fate be an example to you. Dim the lights! Obfuscate! Appeal to passion, not to reason.

A fourth principle of our success is to get them to cover up the battlefield with peace banners, to deny the very existence of the war they're in. This easily follows from the success of the third principle: the Big Lie of relativism. If your philosophy tells you that there are no real absolutes, then there can be no real war. If you reject the idea that there is any real evil worth fighting, and any real good worth fighting for, you reject the idea of fighting, the idea of spiritual warfare itself. What a terrific advantage this gives us on the battlefield: most of our Enemy's troops don't even know it *is* a battlefield.

In the past, our strategy was to get them to vastly *over*estimate our power, fostering fear and terror. That was great fun. But our current strategy is working much better: they so vastly *under*estimate us that they don't even think we exist! We are as invisible to their minds as we are to their eyes.

A wise old military adage said, "Forewarned is forearmed." That is the policy of the hawk. The corollary of this adage is "Unwarned is unarmed." That is the policy of the dove. Result: just put a hawk and a dove together and you see the result.

Our fifth principle is one that has proved effective beyond our wildest dreams. I call it "Satan's Spectacularly Successful Seven-Step Sexual Strategy." Seven S's—the satanically sacred, serpentine letter.

One of their writers seems to have somehow infiltrated our War Room and leaked out the summary strategy sheet, in a book called *Ecumenical Jihad*. Fortunately, he is a minor writer, published by a minor press, and the leaked secret will never get into Borders or Waldenbooks or network TV. We keep careful watch on *those* doors. Here is the summary strategy sheet, in seven steps:

Step 1: The *summum bonum*, the ultimate end, is to win souls for hell. They almost always forget this—the thing the war is ultimately about. We do not. That is our first advantage.

Step 2: One powerful means to this end is the corruption of their society. This works especially well in a society of conformists like them, a society of "other-directed people," especially conformists who think of themselves as noncon-formists.

You see, a good society is simply "a society that makes it easy to be good," in the words of Dorothy Day and Peter Maurin. The satanic corollary is therefore also true: A bad society is a society that makes it easy to be bad. Has there ever been a society in which people have had more and easier opportunities to be bad?

Step 3: The most powerful means to destroy society is to destroy its one absolutely fundamental building block, namely the family. That's the only institution from which most of them ever learn life's most dangerous lesson: unselfish love. It's the only place where they're loved not just for their performance, their doing, but for their being. (If abortion hasn't already ended their being!)

Step 4: The family is best destroyed by destroying *its* foundation: stable marriage.

Step 5: Marriage is destroyed by loosening its glue: sexual fidelity.

Step 6: Fidelity is destroyed by the sexual revolution.

Step 7: And the sexual revolution is propagated mainly by the media, which are now massively in our hands. In fact, the revolution is over, and we've won. There's hardly a single movie made any more that doesn't have some subtle sexual propaganda in it, usually a gratuitous sex scene. And they don't question why; they just gape and lap it up. Duhhhh! Wait till they see the next step!

The simple tactic of getting to their hearts through their hormones has proved incredibly easy. In fact, that's been the main reason they've embraced the Big Lie, denying objective truth. They don't deny objective truth when it comes to sticks and stones, only when it comes to morality. And even in morality, they don't deny objective truth about good and evil when it comes to anything else but sex. They don't defend rape or pillage or slavery or oppression or theft or nuclear war or embezzlement or racism—or even smoking! But they defend divorce and fornication and masturbation and contraception and abortion and sodomy and bestiality and bisexuality and cross-dressing. "Anything goes" is their morality if and only if it has anything to do with sex.

For instance, they don't defend murder, except murder in the name of sex. That name is "abortion," of course. If abortion had nothing to do with sex, we could never have sold it. If storks brought babies, there would be no Planned Parenthood. Abortion is backup birth control, of course, and birth control means the demand to have sex without having babies.

So they are now even willing to murder to defend their so-called sexual freedoms. And to murder the most innocent among them, the *only* innocent among them. And the most tiny and weak and defenseless of all. And in the teeth of nature's strongest instinct: motherhood! A triumph of incredible and undreamed-of proportions.

Oh, we had some notable successes in the past in traveling the hot hormone route, but we never thought it could be a general principle. For instance, back in the sixteenth century we succeeded in dividing England from Rome by attacking Henry the Eighth with our three essential temptations: the world, the flesh and the devil; greed, lust and pride; dynastic ambition, womanizing and resentment at being Poped around. The easiest element to manipulate was lust, of course. *They* like to call the pretty little bastard that resulted "the Church of England," but *we* call it "the Church of Henry's Hormones."[1] Now we've found out how to clone Henry into Kennedys and Clintons, but alas, they don't have any churches in their back pocket for us to pick any more.

But the late twentieth century sexual revolution gave us an effortless solution to an impossible dilemma. Even before the sexual revolution, the sins of the flesh were always easy to tempt them to, but they were clear and obvious sins that made no pretense to be anything else. "Sodomy," "fornication," "pornography," "adultery," "contraception," "prostitution"—these were not nice names. When people sinned, they knew they sinned. We couldn't suppress the scarlet letters, couldn't hide the poison labels. On the other hand, the sins we could and

---

[1] I probably would have edited this offensive insult out if Anglicans didn't have the best sense of humor in Christendom.

did mask very well, the cold, hard sins of arrogance and envy and rage and self-righteousness and wounded pride disguised as honor—these sins were becoming increasingly harder to tempt them to as their political fashions became less elitist and more egalitarian. Well, the sexual revolution solved that problem for us very neatly. It made the easiest sins to tempt them to the most respectable, the most masked by the new philosophy.

And we've masked *that* development from them because they still think the revolution was only a revolution in practice, while it was really a much more radical revolution in philosophy. (The premise again, not just the conclusion, remember?) But those Americans never did pay much attention to philosophy, so they ignored that.

To put the point another way, their sexual practice was always pretty low, but before the revolution, their principles were still fairly high. Now their principles have conformed to their practice instead of vice versa: a perfect example of the Machiavellian principle brought into practice. The principle is that since you can't raise your practice to your principles, you should lower your principles (make them "realistic") to your practice. In this way alone you can avoid hypocrisy, which is the greatest evil.

It's amazing how easily they fell for this packet of fallacies. Of course hypocrisy is not the greatest of all evils, but it's easy to make them think it is because they never think of themselves as hypocrites. And of course hypocrisy doesn't mean not practicing what you preach; hypocrisy means not *believing* what you preach. But it's easy to confuse them about that too, because they don't care much about what you believe, only about what you practice. Finally, if you can't raise your practice to your principles but only lower your principles to your practice, what you have left are not principles at all but just descriptions of practice: isses, not oughts.

What could have dulled their brains so much that they don't see these transparent lies? Sex, of course. So now they not only fornicate, contracept, sodomize and abort; they also justify it, sanctify it and glorify it with Perversion Pride weeks and Sin Satisfaction seminars and Daring Degenerates days. And it feeds on its own success: "Everybody's doing it" becomes a self-fulfilling prophecy. The upshot is that we have killed a bigger enemy than virtue; we've killed conscience, at least in this area.

And since all the virtues are connected, like islands under the sea, our victory in this one area of sex must eventually metastasize. They think they will never become cruel, like their ancestors, only self-indulgent. But they are already cruel, even murderous, to those unborn children who threaten their self-indulgence. They think they cannot be killers, since they are sentimentalists. But the most sentimental nation of all once killed six million of the least sentimental in gas chambers.

Our greatest worry, of course, is the Church of the Enemy's Son. But in the last half century this has been the place of our most surprising victory. Christians abort, fornicate, sodomize, contracept, masturbate and adulterate at exactly the same rate as non-Christians, and most of them don't even know that fact. (Nobody tells them; it would threaten their positive self-esteem!) And if they did know it, they wouldn't know what to do about it. "Just say no" is much too "negative" for them. They have a pathological fear of fear, a phobophobia, a negation of negation.

Why, you may ask, did the sexual strategy work so much

better than any other? How could we get such great mileage out of mere animal weakness, which they have less responsibility for because they have less power and control over it than over the cold, deliberate sins that come from the devil instead of the flesh? How can mere flesh-sin harm them more than spirit-sins?

There are at least seven reasons. For one thing, because it is no longer clear and confessed but is veiled and justified by the new philosophy. *That* is the most dangerous aspect of the sexual revolution to their souls, and they'll never guess it.

Second, because the Enemy thought sex was pretty central. His very first command to them was to "be fruitful and multiply." And he didn't mean "grow oranges and memorize times tables."

Third, sex is their way of originating life itself—in fact, immortal souls. How could that be a mere recreation?

Fourth, it's also an image of the Enemy's own inner life: that one-in-three and two-become-one nonsense they call "love."

Fifth, the Enemy's own Book uses marriage as its main image of the Enemy's plan for them—he actually wants to *join his being with them*, the obscene idiot! And it uses adultery as its main image for the prime sin: unfaithfulness to him. Almost all their major religious metaphors are sexual: "Father" God, "Mother" Church, spiritual "marriage."

Sixth, none of their other appetites is so wildly out of control. Gluttons can't enjoy, or even desire, more than two or three times what they eat, but a single lecher could populate an entire state, and wants to.

Seventh, sex isn't an isolated, partial feature of their lives but pervades everything. If a white man were to wake up one morning and find out that he was the same man, but black, that would be a pretty radical change. If he woke up the same man but twenty years in his future, like Rip Van Winkle, that would also be a pretty radical change. But if he woke up a woman, that would be to him an even more radical change. Change their sex-understanding and you can change their self-understanding.

And the corollaries that follow from the sexual revolution multiply like maggots. Already it is the main motor for the general philosophical revolution into moral relativism and subjectivism and (to justify *that*) epistemological subjectivism ("What is truth?" Forsooth!) and even metaphysical relativism ("Create your own reality")—all from the simple sexual starting point.

It's also produced the greatest generation gap in history. Nothing more sharply separates parents and children than opposite sex ethics. And once the generation gap is widened enough, society is gonzo, without the glue of tradition to hold it together.

Finally, even their science is skewered by their sexism. (What a propaganda triumph *that* term was, by the way!) Evolution is their new dogma because they need it to justify acting like dogs. They ape the apes they think they are. The modern Darwinians are more fanatical and closed-minded than the medieval Aristotelians were. The bishops and the scientists have changed places: it's the scientists who refuse to look through the bishops' telescopes. What fun to watch! They're standing on their heads and they think their critics are upside down.

So here we are, sitting pretty—that is, ugly. What next? More, more, more. Nothing can stop us, and nothing can stop the mudslide, the sweet, sweet sight of civilization swirling down our sinkhole. If the twentieth century was our century, the third millennium will be our millennium.

One little P.S., though, before you party. Not that I want to P.S. on your party, but I need to warn you that something strange seems to be happening. It began in Rome in 1978, when the Enemy corrected his own cardinals by arranging a quick and quiet death for the newly elected Pope John Paul I, a saintly but mild man, and the wholly unexpected election of the saintly but decidedly unmild Pope John Paul II, a formidable warrior who seems to have something up his sleeve for *our* coming millennium. He's a party pooper, and he seems to have some pretty potent poop to pour on our party!

For one thing, he's onto our strategy. He's got to have a spy somewhere in the Lowerarchy. You must find the mole! Triple all tortures! There must be a mole, for the five most remarkable features of this pope for the third millennium exactly match and meet the five newly discovered principles of our strategy for the third millennium that I just outlined. We are no longer taking our Enemy by surprise.

First—the historical point—he's a historical optimist, about youth and the next generation and the future and the third millennium. What does he know, anyway?

He knows the laws of cycles, for one thing, and he knows from experience how strong the Church gets when it's countercultural and persecuted, by Nazis or by Communists. He also knows how weak the Church gets when it's fashionable. He knows the paradox of strong-when-weak and weak-when-strong, as the Enemy's Son taught.

Worse, he seems to know something else, something the saintly but sad popes Pius XII and Paul VI didn't know. Why does he keep talking about the third millennium as if it's going to be *theirs*? I have just proved that it will be *ours*. Yet he speaks as if he knows it will not. It must be false bravado, whistling in the dark. Must be, must be. I mean, our logic is infallible. We have repeatedly checked all our calculations. Where does that old man's smile come from? He has no right to it! It infuriates me! Wipe it away, somebody! How dare he laugh at me? And how dare he write an optimistic encyclical about *our* millennium?

Second, the divide-and-conquer principle seems no longer an automatic gimme. He is the most ecumenical pope in history. He's claiming to begin to reverse the trend of divisions. Of course he can't do that—can he?

Let's think this through. Their primary division began with Luther, especially with his doctrine of justification by faith alone, the nonnegotiable absolute of the Protestants. At the Council of Trent, Rome labeled Lutheranism heretical—and Rome can never go back on a council—and affirmed the necessity of good works as well as faith for salvation. Luther labeled Rome the Antichrist and explicitly denied its theology of salvation. So we have here two different and clearly contradictory answers to the most important question a human can ask: What must I do to be saved? Faith alone, or faith plus good works? One ticket to heaven or two? Logic decrees that no both-and can possibly overcome this either/or.

Yet the Joint Statement on Justification from the Vatican and the German Lutheran bishops, and similar statements from other national bishops' conferences, and statements like Evangelicals and Catholics Together, have now asserted that the core of this issue has been resolved without compromise.

The two churches now perceive that they teach the same truth in substance, though not in terminology. Both ground their teaching in the same data: the New Testament. Returning to their sources seems to have returned them to their senses.

How could we have let this happen? If it can happen to the primary issue, it can happen to any of the others too. The immovable seems to be beginning to move. Could a universal tide be turning? Of course not, of course not, it's impossible. The Humpty-Dumpty principle makes it impossible. But . . . but . . . might that putrid pope-philosopher possibly perceive something we don't?

And our second splitting strategy, our planting modernist spies in all the churches, Protestant and Catholic, seems to be beginning to backfire, because all the orthodox are now uniting against all the modernists. The battle lines are changing. Now most of them see what only a few saw a generation ago: that a biblical Southern Baptist has more in common with the pope than with a modernist Northern Baptist, and that the most Catholic of the Catholic saints are closer to Protestant evangelicals than to Catholic modernists. Modernism was the fundamental heresy of this era, as Gnosticism was of the ancient era. But its very success seems to be turning against us now, if it's uniting the grassroots orthodox in all the churches to oppose it. So in splitting all the churches by planting modernist spies in them, we may have only united all the churches against the spies!

And the third split I mentioned, between Right and Left, between head and heart—well, John Paul confounds our journalists' categories. Anyone so adamant about doctrinal and moral orthodoxy, anyone so stubbornly set against priestesses and abortion and contraception and the sexual revolution, *dare* not be so open and sincere and dialogable and ecumenical. How dare he? He has hijacked our hijack of Vatican II! The journalists who meet him are convinced that he is so human and honest that he must be a secret relativist posing as a dogmatist. Then they are scandalized by his firm dogmatic stands. The journalists who start by scowling at his firm stands are convinced that he must be the Grand Inquisitor posing as a saint, and then they meet him and are bowled over by his sanctity. It was exactly the same with that other rascally reconciler of heart and head, Mother T. She was a lot more formidable than Mister T, let me tell you. She's finally out of our way now—or is she? She threatened to do more from heaven than she ever did from earth. You've got to stop her prayers from getting through; she's spreading herself by dying, as her Master did. Can't anybody get through that angel air force?

The third thing about this pope is that he speaks directly and clearly and forcefully against our masterstroke of relativism. He does not ignore this foundational issue, or speak with mealy mouth about it, as so many of his subordinates do. He does not substitute hate and fear and rhetoric for hard thinking, as the fundamentalists do. He does not compromise with it, as the liberals do. Ooooh, my head still hurts from *Veritatis Splendor!* The very title puts passion and beauty and fire into the concept of truth. He blew our cover to smithereens with that one.

And the Big Lie of relativism, though a bold stroke, is dangerous, because it takes a Ph.D. to be that stupid. Because relativism, of course, is immediately self-contradictory. Is it an absolute that there are no absolutes? How dogmatically we fulminate against dogmatism! Is it objectively true that truth is not objective? We thought we had covered up the logical weakness of our lie by teaching them to scorn logic itself, as if logic were only part of a dead white European male chauvinist conspiracy to oppress women and liberals. But it's becoming increasingly clear to them now that relativism is illiberal, not liberal; totalitarian, not egalitarian; autocratic, not democratic; that when truth is kicked out, power, not compassion, rushes in to take its place.

One of them even discovered "Colson's Law": that cops and conscience are the only two shields against evil—the outer shield and the inner shield. Therefore, insofar as moral relativism softens conscience, it must toughen and multiply cops so that a society of relativists inevitably becomes a police state.

Unfortunately, a police state is a consequence we haven't yet been able to get them to accept. They won't eat just any old food out of our claws yet. We haven't been able to eradicate the Enemy's "natural law" from their hearts and produce "the abolition of man" yet. They still thirst for truth even when surrounded by sophistic philosophies of truthlessness from every side. They still love saints and heroes even when pop psychology has replaced morality in their homilies and families. Even when they no longer *believe* in heroes, they still *love* them. And they still crave beauty, even though our agents of ugliness have dominated nearly every aesthetic establishment of their time. Between liberals, lawyers and liturgists, we thought we had gotten them to despise truth, goodness and beauty. But no. We've not been able to solve the strategic problem of winning their hearts as well as we've won their heads, for though we design most of their philosophies, the Enemy designed their hearts. Anyone who solves that conundrum will be richly rewarded at the banquet below.

Meanwhile, somebody get that big bear off Peter's throne. He fights! And that's our fourth problem: he knows he's at war, and he dares to call our empire "the culture of death." *Evangelium Vitae* is a dangerously passionate call to action, to reevangelize the world. I think he really thinks it can be done! Of course it can't, of course he's a fool, of course. . . . But what the heaven has he got up his sleeve?

In the last decade an amazing number of people have suddenly awakened to the simple fact that they are at war. When Pat Buchanan used the term "culture war" at the 1992 Republican convention, the press demonized him (how I wish *we* could have really demonized him!), and our big media mouths convinced everyone that he wanted to *start* the war, instead of just telling the truth, like the little boy in "The Emperor's New Clothes"—the truth that they're in one. But now, nearly everyone except the media knows he was right, just as they know Dan Quayle was right about Murphy Brown and families.

People are beginning to distrust the experts, our nonsilent minority. They're drawing lines in the sand and defending their families. Home schooling is mega-multiplying. People are even buying dull old books about virtue, because they're getting wise to Colson's Law. They're fighting a holy war, a jihad, and they're doing it together—an ecumenical jihad. And they're joining these two things, ecumenism and jihad, open heart and firm head. They're keeping one hand open to embrace their allies and the other one closed around the hilt of a sword to fight their common enemies, which they're beginning to recognize as us, not each other. So our simple divide-and-conquer strategy that worked for a thousand years seems to be crumbling.

Finally, this pope has countered our Spectacularly Successful Seven-Step Sexual Strategy by an alternative positive
vision, not just no-nos. He's done it by deep and elaborate
theological reflections on the meaning of sex and woman-
hood and manhood and a new theology of the body that poses
a revolutionary threat to our whole sexual revolution with a
dangerous alternative to the traditional matter-versus-spirit
dualism that we've gotten them to swallow for many centuries. And he's done it by things like *Mulieris Dignitatem* ("The
Dignity of Woman"), a title that old bear unfortunately really
believes, especially because of his deep devotion to that horrible woman who actually became the mother of the Enemy's
Son.

So for badness' sake, don't let yourselves be beaten by a
woman! Get those lesbian "feminists" in power fast, before real
femininity comes back into the world and brings the Enemy's
Son down again a million times a day. We can't be beaten by
closed feminist fists and minds, but we can be beaten by open,
Marylike hearts and wombs.

So get out there and fight, you wimps. We will wimp—I
mean, we will win. If only we can figure out why that old man
has that infuriatingly young twinkle in his eye!

6

THE FIERCEST BATTLE
SEX WARS

Most people have heard of the sexual revolution. Many people are even fighting it. (I saw a button on a sad-looking lady that read, "Victim of the Sexual Revolution.") But not many people realize that it is far more revolutionary than any political or military revolution in history, because it changes not just *lives* but *life*—life itself—at its origin. If you think this is exaggeration, read *Brave New World*.

It is a jihad, a holy war, a spiritual struggle. I learned that fact only recently. My teacher was an articulate homosexual activist who was arguing, at Boston College, that "Catholic" and "gay" are as compatible as ham and eggs. I respected the clarity and intelligence of his mind and the openness and apparent goodwill of his heart, so I hoped that our conversation might open and clarify both our minds and teach us something new. (This almost never happens when these two sides argue about this subject.)

I was not disappointed.

I shall try to reconstruct our dialogue with a minimum of additions and polishings, as I like to believe Plato did to Socrates in his early dialogues. For purposes of anonymity, I shall call my dialogue partner "Art."

*   *   *

PETER: Art, I'm really curious about one point of your argument, one part I just don't understand. And I believe in listening before arguing, as you said you do. So I'm not trying to argue now—that's not the point of my question—but first of all to listen and to understand. OK?

ART: Of course. What's the point you don't understand?

PETER: Well, to explain that, I have to ask you to listen too, to where I'm coming from.

ART: And where's that?

PETER: Just the teachings of the Bible and the Church, all of them. I know you don't believe all of them, only some. But I do. So from my point of view, what you do, and what you justify doing, is a sin. That's the label you reject, right?

ART: Right. So what don't you understand?

PETER: Please don't take this as a personal insult, or even an argument, but I know of no other way of phrasing it than with biblical language, which you will probably find offensive. My question is this: Why are you guys the only class of sinners who not only deny that your sin is a sin but insist on identifying yourself with it? We're all sinners, in one way or another,

and I'm not assuming your sins are worse than
mine, but at least I think I'm more than my sins,
whatever they are. I love the sinner but hate the sin.
But you don't, do you?

ART: No, I don't. What I hate is that hypocritical distinction.

PETER: Why?

ART: Because when you attack homosexuality, you attack
homosexuals. It's that simple.

PETER: But alcoholics don't say that the Church attacks
alcoholics when she attacks alcoholism. And cow-
ards don't say that they are their cowardice. And
murderers don't say the Church is hypocritical for
condemning their sin but not them, the sinners.
Adulterers don't deny the distinction between the
adulterer and the adultery. The only group of sinners I've ever heard of who do this is you. And it
seems to me you all do that, you always say that. All
gays say that. Don't they?

ART: Yes, we do. And I forgive you for being so insensi-
tive that you don't realize that you've done right
now what you defend the Church for doing: insult-
ing and rejecting *me*, and not just what I do.

PETER: Wait a minute here! You're saying that when I make
that distinction between what you are and what you
do, when I accept what you are as distinct from what
you do, I'm rejecting what you are? How can I be
rejecting what you are in accepting what you are?

ART: That's exactly what you're doing. In fact, you're trying to kill me.

PETER: What? That's crazy. Now you're being paranoid.

ART: No, listen: In trying to separate what I do from what
          I am, you're trying to separate my body from my
          soul, my sex life from my identity. That's what
          you're doing by insisting on that distinction. Your
          distinction between what you call the "sinner" and
          the "sin" is really death to me; it's the separation of
          body and soul, deed and identity. I'm holding the
          two together; you're trying to pull them apart, and
          that's death.

PETER: That's sophistical. That's an argument that just
          doesn't fit the facts. Look at the facts instead of the
          argument. This is what the Church believes about
          you—what I believe about you: you can be a saint!
          You have dignity. The Church thinks more highly
          of you than you think of yourself. She loves your
          being more than you do; that's why she hates your
          sins against your being. We believe your self is
          greater than your deeds, whatever they are. But you
          don't.

ART: The Church and the Bible tell me I'm an abomina-
          tion to God.

PETER: No! Not in your person, only in your sins, just like
          the rest of us, like all of us. That's Paul's point in
          Romans 1. He's condemning hypocritical condem-
          nation of pagan homosexuals by straight Jews just as
          much as he's condemning pagan homosexuality.

ART: The Church is my enemy.

PETER: The Church is your friend. Because the Church tells
          us two things about you, not just one, and she will
          never change either one, she never can change
          either one, because both are matters of unchange-

able natural law, based on eternal law, based on the very nature of God. She can't ever say that what you do is good for the same reason that she can't ever say that what you are is bad. She defends your being just as absolutely as she attacks your lifestyle; she hates your cancer because she loves your body.

It's the same authority for both. The authority you hate when it condemns what you do is your only reliable ally in defending what you are. You want the Church to change her teaching on what you do, and you're trying to put social pressure on her to do that, but if she did that, then she could change her teaching on what you are, too, for the same reason, under social pressures. I'm sure you know that the old social pressures to hate homosexuals are far from dead. You know what happened in Hitler's Germany. You know how changeable and fickle mankind is—and how dangerous. When the last bastion of absolute moral law is compromised, when even the Church bends to the winds of social pressure, what shelter will you have then?

ART: I'm not worried about the Left; I'm worried about the Right.

PETER: Today, maybe, but what about tomorrow? Today the fashion is to be Leftist, but just a short time ago the fashion was from the Right, and tomorrow it may swing to the Right again, like a pendulum. You can't rely on fashionable opinions to protect you. That's building sandcastles. The tides always change and knock them down.

ART: I'll take my chances, thank you. I don't know what will happen in the future, I grant you that. But I know what's happening now, and I can't take that. We just can't take your "love the sinner, hate the sin" distinction. That much we know.

PETER: You still haven't explained to me why. I began by asking that question, and I really want an answer. I want to know what's going on in your mind.

ART: OK, I think I can explain it to you. You say I shouldn't feel threatened by that distinction, right?

PETER: Right.

ART: You say the Church tells me she loves me, even though she hates what I do, right?

PETER: Right.

ART: Well, suppose the shoe was on the other foot. Suppose *you* were in the minority. Suppose what you wanted to do was to have churches and sacraments and Bibles and prayers, and those in power said to you: "We hate that. We hate what you do. We will do all in our power to stop you from doing what you do. But we love you. We love what you are. We love Christians; we just hate Christianity. We love worshipers; we just hate worship. And we're going to put every possible pressure on you to feel ashamed about worshiping and make you repent of your sin of worshiping. But we love you. We affirm your being. We just reject your doing." Tell me, how would that make you feel? Would you accept their distinction?

PETER: You know, I never thought of it that way. Thank you. You really did make me see things in a new way. You're right. I would not be comfortable with that distinction. I would not be able to accept it. In fact, I would say pretty much what you just said: that you're trying to kill my identity.

ART: See? Now you understand how we feel.

PETER: Yes, I think I do. Thank you very much for showing me that. But do you realize what you've just said? What you've just showed me?

ART: What do you mean?

PETER: You've said to me that sodomy is your religion.

*　　*　　*

At this point Art looked first startled, then thoughtful, as if deciding something. Then he nodded to me with a wry smile and said the following.

*　　*　　*

ART: You were honest with me, so I have to be honest with you. I guess, in a sense, you're right. So now it's my turn to thank you for showing me something. But that doesn't mean you won the argument.

PETER: I didn't think it was an argument. But why have I not won?

ART: Because I'm not ashamed of my religion.

PETER: I am.

ART: You have no right to be ashamed of my religion. Your job is to be ashamed of *your* religion.

PETER: The reason I'm ashamed of yours is that I believe in mine, and mine says that God is ashamed of yours.

ART: *Your* God, maybe.

PETER: No, yours too. There's only one, you know. Haven't you heard that news yet?

ART: If there's only one God, why can't we be one instead
         of arguing?

PETER: No, it's just the opposite: That's why we have to
         argue. If there's only one God, one of us is very
         wrong about him. If there are many gods, if every-
         body has his own god, then everybody can be right.
         So subjectivism and relativism is really polytheism.

*   *   *

Unfortunately, the conversation ended there, as it usually
does when people become too clever. But we both learned
something from it, and that was very unusual.

One of the things I learned was that we cannot win the culture war unless we win the sex war, because sex is the effective religion of our culture, and religion is the strongest force
in the world, the strongest motivation there is.

It shouldn't be surprising that it is sex more than money or
power or fame, because sex is unique. It is holy. It is the only
door by which God himself regularly enters our world to do
the miraculous deed he alone can do: creating new images of
himself. Sex images God because it makes new images of God.

And this is surely why sex is by nature so ecstatic, in both
senses of that word: intensely joyful and self-forgetful. (Ecstasy
literally means "standing outside yourself.") Sex is like religion not only because it is objectively holy in itself but also
because it gives us subjectively a foretaste of heaven, of the
self-forgetful, self-transcending self-giving that is what our
deepest hearts are designed for, long for and will not be satisfied until they have, because we are made in God's own image
and this self-giving constitutes the inner life of the Trinity.

Thus it is no accident that our culture's deepest and most

shocking moral defeat is abortion. Nothing less than a false religion could so overcome the natural moral law and nature's deep instinct of motherhood. Abortion is a religious issue not just because traditional religions happen to oppose it but because abortion is necessarily about sex. As was pointed out above, a woman (or more usually, the man!) wants abortion only because she wants to have sex without babies.

So in order to fully persuade the people in our society that abortion is not an option, that babies are holy and not to be treated as toys to be thrown away at will, we must achieve a much harder task: we must persuade them that sex is holy and not to be treated as a toy. For sex is the context of abortion. Abortion is different from other issues because sex is different from other issues.

The surrounding context is always the most powerful determining factor: if you can surround an enemy in battle or the shooter in basketball or the king on a chessboard, you will win. If you surround a choice with truth and light, then that choice will be a right one. If you surround it with darkness, it will be a wrong one. If you surround an individual with a good family and a good society, that individual will find it easy to make right choices. If you surround him with a broken family and a broken society, wrong choices will be easy and natural. So if you surround a hard choice (abortion, homosexuality, pornography) with the truth about the holy mystery of sex, as society used to do (at least significantly better than today), then even ordinary people will make the right choices.

Pope John Paul II's theology of the body, perhaps his greatest contribution to posterity, is the positive alternative to modernity's two false and destructive philosophies of the body: the dehumanizing materialization and objectification of it by scientific positivism, and the idolatrous spiritualization and subjectivization of it by the Gnosticism of the sexual revolution. Whenever the world produces a heresy, the Church produces a doctrine. Whenever the world produces a lie, the Church defines a truth. Whenever the world produces great sinners, the Church produces great saints.

According to the teaching of the Roman Catholic Church, the Church is not limited to the Roman Catholic Church. (Father Feeny was excommunicated for teaching that.) In battling the sexual revolution and its primary sacrament of abortion, evangelical Protestants have been in the front line of the battle together with orthodox Catholics. What they have in common is a refusal to correct the Bible, their written marching orders from General God. Liberal mainline Protestants and liberal Catholics straggle together in the foggy rear, unwilling to even use the biblical imagery of spiritual warfare. The battle lines are becoming clearer to all, and so are the lines defining the identity of the Church.

*   *   *

All right, then, what do we do about it? Now that we understand that sex functions as a religion, how does that help us win the culture war?

Most of the answers concern how we think, because that is the source and strength of what we do.

1. Be realistic. Don't expect the victims of the sexual revolution to be objective and rational. You are challenging their god. You are waging spiritual warfare. You are condemning their ecstasy.

2. Always put the negatives (no to sins) in the context of the positives (yes to sinners).

3. Make clear (first of all to yourself) the *reason* sex is holy: like conversion and like the Eucharist, it brings God himself to earth. Conception is a divine act, a miracle.

4. Recognize and affirm the presence of genuine human love even in sinful relationships. Human motives are usually mixed, and very unholy things are sometimes done with almost holy intentions or with intentions in which charity and cupidity, love and lust, are closely and confusedly intertwined, like cancer cells and healthy cells.

5. Use your imagination. Remember, "there but for the grace of God go I." Suppose you were confused and victimized by a sexual perversion. Suppose you got your heavenly ecstasy only from porcupines or Venus flytraps. Invoke the Golden Rule: what would you most deeply want the Church to do for you? You would want the Church to deliver you, certainly, rather than either simply condemning or simply condoning your perversion. But how? What kind of deliverance? Decide this, then "go and do likewise" (Luke 10:37).

6. Make heroic sacrifices for the spiritually poor, the enslaved. Be a humble and anonymous hero of purity and chastity. Sacrifice your "freedom of thought" first of all. "Take every thought captive to obey Christ" (2 Corinthians 10:5). In other words, "Don't even think about it," or about yourself. Do it simply for the love of God and God's lost children.

When a body is threatened by a disease, it produces antibodies to fight the disease like soldiers, giving themselves up for the survival of the body. The body of Christ is a real body, and therefore it too produces antibodies: saints. The antibodies are tailored to the disease. If the body is threatened with the disease of greed, the body produces heroes of poverty, like St. Francis. If threatened with the disease of indifference to human life, the body produces missionaries of charity, like Mother Teresa. If threatened with the disease of violence, the body produces heroes of nonviolence. If it is gluttony, it produces heroes of fasting. If drunkenness, heroes of sobriety.

In fact, *all* these diseases deeply afflict our world, and therefore the body of Christ must produce antibodies to combat all of them. The newest and most critical ones today seem to be the sexual diseases, but the old ones are still just as serious as they always were, and there is desperate need for volunteers to fight in all these areas of the battlefield.

The crucial common feature of all these antibodies is that they are not just sin avoiders but saints; not just good people but little Christs, hands and fingers of Christ, whose imperfect and human sacrifices constitute some of the medicines that the Great Physician, in his strange, divine wisdom, chooses to use to save his world.

7

THE SECRET
WEAPON THAT WILL
WIN THE WAR

SAINTS

T he strongest weapon in the world is sanctity. Nothing can defeat it.

It may sound strange to some people to speak of sanctity in connection with warfare, even spiritual warfare. Many "religious people" like to think about sanctity because they think it is just the opposite of war. They think it is not only peaceful but "nice": comforting, upbeat, happifying.

They are wrong. Christ is indeed the Prince of Peace, but the peace Christ gives is radically distinctive. It is given "not as the world gives" (see John 14:27). And it certainly is not "nice." Perhaps the popular conception of saints is "nice," but real saints are not nice. They are warriors. They really bother people, so deeply that they are often martyred. If they don't bother anybody, they are not saints. That is what Jesus said: "If they persecuted me, they will persecute you" (John 15:20). You don't take nice people and nail them to a cross. Do we judge Jesus by our "nice" idea of what a saint should be, or do we judge our idea of what a saint is by the data of Jesus?

Why is Jesus' peace so different from any peace the world can give us? Because the world can give us peace with itself, the flesh and the devil, while Jesus gives us peace with neighbor, self and God. The world gives us a peace based on greed and lust and pride: greed for the things of the world, lust for the things of the flesh and pride for the things of the devil. But Jesus gives us a peace based on poverty, chastity and obedience—the three weapons that directly fight greed, lust and pride. In fact, the two kinds of peace are at war with each other. Saints understand that.

The world thinks, rightly, that saints are masters of love and, wrongly, that love is nice. The love Jesus came to give is as distinctive as the peace he came to give, and he explicitly said that. He said that the whole world would be able to distinguish Christians from everyone else by the different kind of love they had. (John 13:35: "By this everyone will know that you are my disciples, if you have love for one another.") If this love were not distinctive, how could the world distinguish Christians from everyone else by their love?

Saints love true peace. They also hate false peace, peace based on lies. Saints hate violence and intolerance against sinners. But they also hate tolerance of sin. Saints love sinners more, and sins less, than anyone else does. Both of these eccentricities puzzle people and often offend them.

In Jesus' day, the first of these two things saints do—loving sinners—offended his enemies, for the fashion was then rather overcruel: a truth without peace. Today, the second of these two things saints do—hating sins—offends the enemies of Christ and his Church, for the fashion now is rather overkind: a peace without truth.

In Jesus' day, those who loved sinners were accused of loving sins. Today, those who hate sins are accused of hating sinners. Anyone who speaks against sodomy is accused of "homophobia." Soon, to speak against fornication or even adultery may be labeled sexophobia. Already, to speak out against abortion is called "divisive" and "judgmental." In places in Canada and even the United States, to merely state the Church's perennial teachings, and Christ's, on controversial issues of sexual morality is illegal; it is "hate speech."

Saints are not nice. They are embroiled in controversy, necessarily, always. This is because saints are as devoted to truth as they are to love; they will not be false prophets who give the people what they want instead of what they need.

But no matter how unpopular the job description of the saint may be, their double devotion to truth and love is the only weapon that can win the war against the culture of death. Only saints can save the world.

The deepest reason why the Church is weak and the world is dying is that there are not enough saints.

No, that's not quite honest. The reason is that *we* are not saints.

Can you imagine what ten more Mother Teresas would do for this world? Or ten more John Wesleys? No, you can't imagine it, any more than anyone could imagine how twelve nice Jewish boys could conquer the Roman Empire. You can't imagine it. But you can do it. You can become a saint.

Absolutely no one and nothing can stop you. It's your totally free choice. Here is one of the most wonderful and terrifying sayings I have ever read (from William Law's *Serious Call to a Devout and Holy Life*): "If you will look into your own heart in utter honesty, you must admit that there is one and only one reason why you are not, even now, as saintly as the primitive Christians: you do not wholly want to be."

That insight is terrible because it is an indictment, but at the same time it is wonderful and hopeful because it is also an offer, an open door. Each of us can become a saint. We really can. *We really can.* I say it three times because I think we do not really believe it. For if we did, how could we endure being anything less?

What holds us back, then?

Fear. Fear of paying the price.

What is the price?

The answer is simple. T. S. Eliot gave it when he defined the condition of being a Christian as costing everything. The price is everything you have. Give Christ one hundred percent of your heart and life one hundred percent of the time, holding nothing back, absolutely nothing at all, anywhere, ever. This means martyrdom—and for most of us, a more extended and difficult martyrdom than that of the noose or execution block. It means the martyrdom of dying daily, dying every minute for as long as you live, dying to all your desires and plans, including your pet plans about how to become a saint.

Or rather—to be more theologically and psychologically exact—not dying to your desires (Christ does not want desireless wimps) but dying to the "you" in your desires. This sounds much more mystical than it is. It simply means giving

God a blank check and letting him fill in the amount. It means "islam," complete submission, surrender, *fiat*—Mary's thing. Look at what Mary's thing did two thousand years ago when she did it: it brought God down from heaven and saved the world.

It was meant to continue.

If we do that Mary-thing, that "islam," and only if we do that, then all our apostolates will work, our preaching and teaching and writing and catechizing and missioning and mothering and fathering and nursing and businessing and pastoring and priesting—everything. The human soul is a tube, like a tunnel connecting two places, heaven and earth. If the tube is open and empty and hungry at the heavenly end, to suck grace in, then and only then will the tube be full like a cornucopia at the earthly end to pour grace out.

Last year an American Catholic bishop commissioned one of the priests of his diocese to write up recommendations for ways to increase the number of men seeking to fulfill a clerical vocation. The priest was young but wise and holy. He concluded his report this way: "The best way to attract men in this diocese to the priesthood, Your Excellency, would be your canonization." When we see a saint, we know the purpose of our own lives. Saints reproduce themselves simply by being what they are.

So why can't you be canonized—become a saint?

But how? We always want to know how. We are the know-how people. We want a method, a technology. Let's examine that want. What is a method, a technique or a technology? It is a means to an end. So we want a means to the end of sanctity. Now a means is something easy, like pressing a button, to an end that is something hard, like lighting up a room or bringing enough energy to a rocket to lift it off the earth. We do not use a means that is harder than an end: we do not travel around the world and gather burning lava and bring it back into our house in order to light up the living room So "a means to the end of sanctity" means something that is easier than sanctity and that will cause sanctity, so that if we do this something, or attain this something, then this something will be the middle term, the link between us and sanctity.

And there is no such thing. No prayer, no meditation, no yoga, no twelve-step program, no psychological trick or device or technique. No technique at all. There is no button for sanctity, any more than there is a button for love. For sanctity *is* love, charity, loving God with all your heart and sou₁ and mind and strength and your neighbor as yourself. How do you love? *You just do it.* A cause cannot produce an effect greater than itself. And nothing is greater than sanctity, nothing is greater than love. Therefore no cause, no human cause, can produce sanctity. There is no technology for sanctity.

Of course God is its cause, grace is its cause, the Holy Spirit is its cause.

Well, why doesn't he cause it, then? If only God's grace can make us saints, why doesn't God give us the grace and make us saints?

Because he is a gentleman and respects our freedom, giving us only what we truly want, and we don't really want it. If we really wanted it, we'd get it. Insofar as we want it, we get it. For this "it," namely sanctity, is itself a matter of wanting. There is no gap between the wanting and the getting. As soon as we want it, we have it, because "it" is sanctity, and sanctity is loving, and loving is willing, and willing is wanting.

It's embarrassingly simple. We have been promised, by

God incarnate, that all who seek, find. In other words, "just say yes," "just do it."

It's infinitely simple, and that's why it's hard. The hard part of the formula "just say yes" is the first word: "just." We are comfortable with Christ and ourselves, or Christ and our theology, or Christ and our psychology, or Christ and our country, or Christ and our politics, or Christ and culture, or Christ and counterculture; but just plain Christ, Christ drunk straight and not mixed, is far too dangerous for us. We know that "Aslan is not a tame lion." If you just say yes to *him*, you don't know *what* he'd do to you.

Yet this thing we fear is our only winning weapon. If we use this weapon, we will win this war, and if we do not use this weapon, we will not win this war. More exactly, insofar as we use this weapon, we will win this war, and insofar as we do not, we will not.

And the war, remember, is not just for society but for souls, not just for this time but for eternity.

8

BASIC TRAINING
HOW TO BE A SAINT

How do we get the weapon that alone will win the war? How do we become saints? We did not answer this question in the previous chapter, except to say that there is no means, no technology, no method for it.

To explore this question, I will now share with you (fashionable euphemism for "impose upon you") the following dream, even though people who tell us their dreams probably annoy us more than anyone else, next to mimes.

In my dream I got to ask just one question of my guardian angel. (For those of you who are ignorant of angelology, one of the most practical of all human sciences, angels know far more than we do because they have a kind of limited but real mental telepathy with God.) I chose the question of how to become a saint because it is the most practical question I could imagine for each individual and for human society, especially today, and also because I thought it would involve many other questions, thus keeping my angel around for a long while. (I wanted to keep him around as long as I could because it is a far more wonderful privilege to hang around angels than to hang around the greatest human sages of all time. This is one of the things we have to look forward to in heaven.)

In the ensuing dialogue, I put my angel's words in common typeface, as befitting an angel of great common sense, and mine in thin, rightward-leaning italics, as befitting a skinny semiconservative.

*   *   *

ANGEL: Hail, Peter. [Angels say "hail," not "hi."] I have been allowed to speak with you directly for a few minutes, though only in a dream. Our common Commanding Officer will not tell you why, and he does not want you to guess. I have been sent to test you, not by asking questions but by answering them. You will meet the test if you ask one good question.

PETER: *Then I will ask this one. Tell me about the "pearl of great price," the "one thing needful."*

ANGEL: Good. What do you want to know about it?

PETER: *What it is and how to attain it.*

ANGEL: You already know what it is. It's no secret. You know Leon Bloy's great line: "Life offers only one tragedy, in the end: not to have been a saint."

PETER: *Yes, I know. That's why I want to know how to do that.*

ANGEL: The answer to that question is also no secret. It's a matter of public record.

PETER: *Public record?*

ANGEL: God has told us, in ten words.

PETER: *You mean his commandments?*

ANGEL: Indeed. Do you know them?

PETER: *Of course.*

ANGEL: Can you recite them?

PETER: *I thought I was supposed to ask the questions.*

ANGEL: When a man gives excuses for not doing something, the time has come to do that thing.

PETER: *Well, now, let's see...*

ANGEL: There's no need to waste time. I see your mind has a muddled and only semiaccurate memory of them. It would be far better to memorize them, you know. You do *not* know them well enough to justify your first answer: "Of course." They should be an "Of course"; they are in fact only a "Well, now, let's see." But at least you know clearly the point and sum of all of them. For every Jew has known this since Moses: "Hear, O Israel: The LORD is our God, the LORD alone. You shall love the LORD your God with all your heart, and with all your soul, and with all your might."

PETER: *So it's all or nothing.*

ANGEL: In the end, yes, though it takes time to get to the end. But God is infinitely patient and infinitely demanding. As George MacDonald put it, he is "easy to please but hard to satisfy."

PETER: *And until then?*

ANGEL: You keep practicing the dance until you get it perfect.

PETER: *But I give up so easily. I'm a terrible dancer. I call it quits after one fall.*

ANGEL: But it's not only up to you; it's up to him, and he's a bulldog, a Churchill, a fanatic. He never gives up.

PETER: *"Our Fanatic who art in heaven . . ."*

ANGEL: Father, Lover, Fanatic: they're almost synonymous. His Word never calls him a grandfather or an uncle.

PETER: *Doesn't it also use some less personal images that are a little less formidable?*

ANGEL: Less formidable? Like a "consuming fire"? No, no, don't tilt your head and slit your eyes at me like that. It's his résumé, not mine. I just deliver his mail.

PETER: *So what do I do now?*

ANGEL: You get on with it. Fulfill the purpose of your existence. Finish the grand drama your Father in heaven invented and for which he banged out the Big Bang and waited 15 billion years and evolved dinosaurs and moved all worlds. Bring the universe to completion. Say yes. Be a saint.

PETER: *Wait! Don't go! I have one more question.*

ANGEL: That's your problem.

PETER: *But this one must be divinely inspired, because it comes from the lyrics of an old Broadway song.*

ANGEL: That's as absurd an argument as I've ever heard. But I have a special thing for old Broadway lyrics, so I'll answer this one question more. What is it?

PETER: *The line is "All of me—why not take all of me?" God knows that's what I want most of all: for him to take all of me, not just part. Why doesn't he do to the rest of me what he's done to part of me?*

ANGEL: Because he's a lover, not a thief. He takes only what you give.

PETER: *Then why doesn't he make me give him all of me?*

ANGEL: Love does not *make* you do anything. Love does not rape; love seduces.

PETER: *I know, I know. But why doesn't he seduce me more?*

ANGEL: Have you asked him?

PETER: *Of course.*

ANGEL: How?

PETER: *I pray, "Let me give you all of me."*

ANGEL: He's not stopping you.

PETER: *But I know I can't do it without his grace. I know it's only by his grace that I've been able to give him those little bits of me that I have given him so far, so it's got to be only by his grace that I will ever give him all of me.*

ANGEL: You're right there.

PETER: *So the very act of my giving all of me to him—that very act is his act, his gift, his grace.*

ANGEL: It's his grace, but it's your act.

PETER: *So why doesn't he give me the grace?*

ANGEL: He did. He does. He will.

PETER: *Then why isn't it effective? Why don't I give him all of me?*

ANGEL: That's the question you have to answer by your will, your choices, not by your mind.

PETER: *Has he given me enough grace?*

ANGEL: Yes.

PETER: *Then have I not received it?*

ANGEL: You have received it in its fullness. Its name is Christ. It is a "him," not an "it."

PETER: *Then why am I not a saint?*

ANGEL: You already know the answer: because you do not wholly want to be.

PETER: *But I want to wholly want to be!*

ANGEL: Yes, but you do not *wholly* want to wholly want to be.

PETER: *This sounds like an et cetera et cetera ad infinitum.*

ANGEL: It is not a logical puzzle. It is solvable only by your will, not by your mind. No explanation will help; no road map will make you move.

PETER: *That sounds pretty hopeless.*

ANGEL: Not at all. Look at yourself. Have you ever moved? Have you grown at all?

PETER: *So little.*

ANGEL: But a little.

PETER: *Yes.*

ANGEL: So you are growing. You are a spiritual infant. Christ is not yet mature in you.

PETER: *And that is my fault.*

ANGEL: That is also your destiny. Do not feel guilty about your very being. God did not design you to become a saint in one day. You must not try to go faster than grace, and grace proportions itself to nature. You know the maxim of the medieval philosophers: "Whatever is received, is received according to the mode of the receiver." And the mode of any creaturely receiver is *time.* Your nature is to be like a plant, not a machine. God is your gardener, not your mechanic. When his supreme gift, his own Son, entered time, even he began as a baby and grew slowly in grace (Luke 2:52). What happened in that stable must happen in your soul.

PETER: *I think I understand. It is his gift, his grace, but there are conditions. There are strings attached.*

ANGEL: What a strange way to describe the ontological

nature of things! If his gift were a ball, would you say that the roundness of the ball was "strings attached"? Or that nature itself was the strings attached to grace?

PETER: I *am confused. I always wondered about the relation between nature and grace.*

ANGEL: That is because you have hypostatized both.

PETER: *What do you mean?*

ANGEL: You have thought of them as *things*. They are not separate things. Nature is simply the nature of grace, the form grace takes when it is received in time.

PETER: *Is that why he doesn't do instant miracles most of the time?*

ANGEL: Yes.

PETER: *But he does do that some of the time.*

ANGEL: Yes. Miracles are what you would call the exceptions that prove the rules of nature. What you really mean to say in that confused saying is that they are the exceptions that *presuppose* the rules.

PETER: *And "the rules" here include time and growth.*

ANGEL: Yes.

PETER: *I like the exceptions better than the rules. When he does a miracle, I say to myself, I love it when he does stuff like that!*

ANGEL: Liking only the exceptions and not the rules is self-contradictory, you know. You can't even believe in miracles unless you believe in the laws of nature, the rules that define the miracles as exceptions.

PETER: *I know. I accept the rules.*

ANGEL: Why?

PETER: *Because they are his. Because they are his will.*

ANGEL: That is a very good beginning to becoming a saint.

PETER: *It sounds awfully prosaic.*

ANGEL: Of course. Being a saint is the most prosaic thing in the world.

PETER: *Is it not the most poetic thing in the world?*

ANGEL: It is that too.

PETER: *When shall I taste the poetry? When shall I see the face of God?*

ANGEL: In due time.

PETER: *You sound like my father. He used to say that.*

ANGEL: Both your father and I sound like God. God always says that.

PETER: *So are you telling me I should be more patient?*

ANGEL: Yes, that too.

PETER: *Well, that's one of the things I am very impatient for: the gift of patience. I'm in a bind.*

ANGEL: It's not a bind. It's a gift, a grace.

PETER: *Impatience is a gift?*

ANGEL: Yes. Haven't you read Job?

PETER: *Yes.*

ANGEL: It worked for him.

PETER: *I thought patience was a virtue and a gift.*

ANGEL: It is.

PETER: *But aren't patience and impatience contradictory? Doesn't patience mean waiting for God's time?*

ANGEL: No, they're not contradictory. And yes, patience means waiting for God's time. But God's time is now. God's time is always now.

PETER: *So I should give "all of me" to God in his time, and his time is now, so I should give him "all of me" now.*

ANGEL: You know that syllogism is valid and that conclusion is true.

PETER: *What about the future and process and growth?*

ANGEL: If the plant does not grow in the present, it will not grow more in the future.

PETER: Oh. *I think I understand.*

ANGEL: I have a suggestion for you.

PETER: *What?*

ANGEL: Don't think. Don't understand. Just do it. Do it now, instead of thinking about doing it later. It takes time to think, and time to understand, but it takes no time at all to do it.

PETER: *I see.*

ANGEL: No, don't see it; do it.

PETER: Oh. *I don't know what to say to that.*

ANGEL: Don't say anything. Don't say it; do it.

PETER: *I will. I will.*

ANGEL: No, don't will it; do it. Willing it means planning to do it in the future instead of doing it now. If you did it, you wouldn't have to will it; you'd just do it.

PETER: *Is that your answer to my question?*

ANGEL: What question?

PETER: *The question is "How do I give all of me?" And your answer is "Just do it"?*

ANGEL: That's not my answer; that's God's commandment. He's the one who's really asking the questions, you know, not you. It's all in Job. How quickly you forget what you know!

PETER: *I'm confused. I don't know what to think.*

ANGEL: Don't think. Just do it.

PETER: *I see: I'm an absent-minded professor who thinks too much. It's a comfortable substitute for doing. I see my mistake.*

ANGEL: Even seeing your mistake is only seeing and another substitute for doing. Even seeing that seeing is a substitute for doing still doesn't turn seeing into doing. Nothing does.

PETER: *How persistent you are!*

ANGEL: And how persistent *you* are in running away. I don't want compliments, and God doesn't want A's on his tests; he wants your heart. He's your lover, not your professor.

PETER: *I am a fool.*

ANGEL: Yes, you are, but even that is a distraction now. You are playing games. But there is serious work to be done. Stop trying to distract me. It can't be done.

PETER: *I give up. I surrender.*

ANGEL: It's about time. Now we can begin. Put away your toys, child. Come home. Look your Father full in the face. That is the crucial thing.

PETER: *The crucial thing in becoming a saint?*

ANGEL: Yes. Because no one can sin while looking him in the face.

PETER: *Because his face is goodness?*

ANGEL: Because his face is truth. Total honesty with the truth is the key to holiness.

PETER: *So it's the intellect rather than the will that determines all? It's the mind that is primary?*

ANGEL: No. It's the will. Because you must *will* the light You must *choose* to turn your face to his. Everything follows from that choice.

PETER: *And what prevents us from making that choice?*

ANGEL: Many things. Too many to tell. You cannot kill all the gnats that distract you. You must simply ignore them. But you should be aware of the biggest one. That is pride. You want to do it your way. You want control. That is why I began to give you these direct answers only when you uttered the magic words "I give up." And I will continue to do so forever. I am the Father's servant, and therefore yours, forever.

PETER: I *am truly under the Mercy.*

9

THE PROGNOSIS
FOR VICTORY

WHY WE MUST WIN

The cost may be great, and the time may be long, but the outcome cannot be in doubt. Three nonnegotiables, three absolutes, make that necessary. If there is any wisdom in the world, this is it, these three reasons why God's people must win the culture war.

1. Because truth is stronger than falsehood, light is stronger than darkness. Whenever light shines into darkness, the darkness cannot comprehend it: it cannot understand it, cannot surround it and cannot put it out.

2. Because love is stronger than hate, and we fight because we love God and man and nature and children and femininity and masculinity and sexuality and the body and the soul and life and love and truth, while the enemy does not. Love is

even stronger than death; it is certainly stronger than hate.

"God is love [*agape*], and those who abide in love abide in God, and God abides in them" (1 John 4:16). God cannot lose, and God is love, therefore if we abide in love, we cannot lose—and if we do *not* abide in love, we *ought* to lose.

3. Because Jesus is Lord, Christ is King—and this is not a mythic image from a primitive politics or a nice idea for having a nice day or an "ideal" to motivate a human striving, but it is an eternally necessary fact next to which the galaxies look like gossamer.

We will win because we wield the world's most unconquerable weapon, the strongest force in the universe. To translate it from the abstract to the concrete, the weapon is the blood of Christ. Not Christ without blood, not merely a beautiful ideal; and not blood without Christ, not a merely human sacrifice and martyrdom. Christ's blood. The blood that saved the world two thousand years ago still flows and still accomplishes the same work. Insofar as we let ourselves be Christ's blood bank, we will save our society and our world.

Back in the 1950s and 1960s, when there were still more Communists in Russia than in American universities, Archbishop Fulton Sheen used to say that Russia was like the cross without Christ and that America was like Christ without the cross. Neither sacrifice without love nor love without sacrifice will win. And neither will work. But the blood of Christ will work, for that blood flows from his sacred heart, and the heart of that heart is *agape*, divine love, and *agape* never gives up. Love never gives up.

And that is why we will never give up and why we will win, we whose food is this blood. And that will be our last point: the absolute confidence that we must win this war. We must remember this point, for otherwise we may despair of attaining such a high ideal as sanctity.

The hard-nosed, successful secular lawyer Gerry Spence writes, "A small boy and a bully meet. When the small boy is knocked down, he gets up and attacks again, over and over, until at last he will win. Nothing in the world is as fearsome as a bloody, battered opponent who will *never* surrender."

Winston Churchill delivered the shortest and most memorable commencement speech of all time at his alma mater during World War II. Its most memorable line was: "Never, never, never, never, never, never, never, never, never give up."

We will win the war because no matter how many times we fall down, no matter how many times we fail at being saints, no matter how many times we fail at love, we will never, never, never give up.

We will win because we are the body of Christ, and Christ is God, and God is love, and love never, never, never gives up.